THE
EXTRAORDINARY
EXIT

THE
EXTRAORDINARY
EXIT

How to Sell Your Business for
Maximum Value, Protect Your Legacy,
and Walk Away *with* No Regrets

ANDY HARRIS &
JONATHAN SHERRILL

Cheval Press

THE EXTRAORDINARY EXIT
How to Sell Your Business for Maximum Value, Protect
your Legacy, and Walk Away with No Regrets
First Edition

ISBN   978-1-967509-07-2   *Hardcover*
       978-1-967509-06-5   *Paperback*
       978-1-967509-05-8   *eBook*
       978-1-967509-08-9   *Audiobook*

LCCN   2025924719

CONTENTS

DEDICATION

JONATHAN

To my wife, Dana, and my daughter, Faith—you are my why. Selling my business was never about getting the maximum valuation; it was about creating the freedom and security you both deserve. Your love, strength, and support have been the foundation of every decision, and I thank God every day for you.

To God, for guiding my steps, even when the path was difficult. His faithfulness has been evident through every challenge and transition, and I am grateful beyond measure for His everlasting love.

And to every entrepreneur, founder, and business owner who has poured their life into building something meaningful—this book is for you. I know your exit isn't just a transaction; it's the culmination of your sacrifice, risk, and vision. May it be everything you've dreamed of: amazing, significant, and worthy of your journey.

ANDY

To my wife, Stephanie, and our daughters, Hannah and Georgia, for their love, support, and patience with me throughout my career, and for allowing me to serve others and be away from home as much as I was.

To God, for giving me the belief, trust, faith, and skills I needed to take the high road on the journey through life and business.

To all the team members who have helped me and the businesses/communities we serve achieve great success.

To the mentors who have guided me and our teams to live with purpose and trust in your "why" to lead you through the lowest valleys to the highest peaks, and everything in between.

To the entrepreneurs and business owners who are looking for an Extraordinary Exit from the business they've poured their lives into—one where they achieve maximum valuation and get all of their desired outcomes, and ultimately fulfill their "why."

And to Rob Follows and STS Capital Partners, for giving me the opportunity to help entrepreneurs and private business owners achieve significance through the sale of their business.

FOREWORD

At seventeen, my life flipped upside down.

My dad owned a small men's clothing store in Canada, and one day, he had to declare bankruptcy. It was crushing. But as hard as that experience was, it planted the seeds of who I am today.

That store was my first taste of business. I started working there at twelve and, before long, I was the top salesperson. Eventually, the other employees started complaining that I was "causing too much drama," mainly because I kept asking questions. So my dad fired me.

That was almost fifty years ago. And guess what?

I'm still asking questions.

Because questions are the foundation of extraordinary results.

It was my curiosity—my relentless need to learn—that led me to discover the power of coaching. That discovery changed everything. It helped me build and sell companies worth hundreds of millions of dollars. It helped me win Ernst & Young's Entrepreneur of the Year award and the Blue Chip Enterprise Award for overcoming adversity. It helped me complete twelve full-distance Ironman triathlons, including five Hawaii World Championships. And it helped me become a US National Squash Champion.

More importantly, it led me to build CEO Coaching International, where for the past seventeen years, we've coached over 1,500 CEOs and leadership teams to achieve extraordinary growth. On average, companies that have worked with us for two years or more have grown revenue at nearly three times the US average and EBITDA at over four times the national benchmark.

How do they do it?

They surround themselves with world-class coaches who ask the right questions—and then they do the work to implement the right answers.

I share this because asking questions and seeking the right guidance has created ripple effects for thousands of people, myself included. That's why I believe so strongly in coaching. A coach keeps you accountable to specific, measurable actions that drive results. A coach gives you the perspective to see blind spots and the experience to accelerate growth.

And when it comes time to sell your company, a coach can help you get from six-figure revenues to nine-figure exits.

Andy Harris and Jonathan Sherrill understand this, too.

I first met Andy when he joined YPO back in 2010, and the firm he works for, STS Capital Partners®, has been a strategic partner of CEO Coaching International for years. Jonathan worked with one of our coaches while leading Quicken Steel. That partnership helped him step out of the day-to-day whirlwind, focus on what really moves the needle, and lock in on the levers that drive profitability and scale.

Both Andy and Jonathan know that no one wins alone. The right insights, the right perspective, and the right support can make the difference between an average outcome and a life-changing one.

This book is about making your exit life-changing.

Inside these pages, Andy and Jonathan have distilled decades of experience into actionable strategies to help you avoid common pitfalls, maximize your company's valuation, and navigate the complex world of selling your business. It's not just about the transaction—it's about setting yourself up for a successful next chapter.

At CEO Coaching International, our mission is simple: empower leaders to build life-changing businesses and live extraordinary lives. It's clear that Andy and Jonathan share that same goal.

If you're thinking about selling, don't do it alone.

Read this book. Apply what you learn. Surround yourself with people who've done it before—because life's too short for small results.

Make *Big* Happen!

—MARK MOSES

CEO of CEO Coaching International

INTRODUCTION

ALMA

7:00 a.m., Friday morning

Alma sat at her breakfast table, slowly sipping her tea. It should have been a day of triumph, but instead, she felt...empty. No, it was worse than that. She felt *defeated*. Full of regret. She had just closed on a deal to sell the business she had spent two decades building, and all she could think was, *I made a mistake*.

During due diligence, the buyer found problems Alma hadn't anticipated. As a result, they dropped their offer price and added earnouts to the deal structure. After months of presentations, answering questions about her company, and responding to the buyer's requests for more information, she had been exhausted. She just didn't have the energy to keep going, let alone go through the process again, so she agreed to the lower price and the less favorable terms.

Sitting at the table that morning, it felt like all the blood, sweat, and tears she had poured into her company were for nothing. When she started the process, she thought the sale was going to set her up for the next adventure, whatever that turned out to be. She thought it was going to provide her with the kind of financial security she had always dreamed about. But she was wrong.

Alma wished she could go back in time—if she could, she would do things very differently. For one thing, she would have started preparing her company for the sale well before they actually went to market. She would have gotten clear on *why* she wanted to sell, and she would have found a dedicated sell-side advisor to represent her.

Sighing, she stared out the window, one thought circling around and around in her head: *Now what am I supposed to do?*

CHARLES

7:00 a.m., Friday morning

Charles sat at his breakfast table, coffee mug in hand. But instead of rushing through a hurried breakfast before heading into his office the way he usually did, he lingered over his coffee, savoring every drop.

While he sipped his coffee, he replayed the events of the previous day in his mind. He recalled the smiles on the buyers' faces as they all shook hands. He remembered the elation he felt when his leadership team congratulated him on the sale, and as he listened to their excitement about what the future held. And he thought about how it had felt when he got the confirmation that the funds had been wired.

He had done it. With the help of a great sell-side advisor, a stellar legal team, and his longtime coach, he had sold his business—the one he'd dedicated the last twenty years of his life to growing—for a price that was more than *three times* his initial expectations. The deal delivered everything else he wanted, too. The buyer was a strategic who wanted to take the company to new heights, and they were committed to doing right by his employees and his customers.

His wife looked over at him. "This is the happiest I've seen you look in a while," she said, smiling at him.

He nodded, then stood up to give her a big hug. He *was* happy. Euphoric, in fact. Starting his business and growing it had been deeply fulfilling, of course. But this feeling...it was incomparable. He had found the perfect home for his business and his employees, and now he and his family were financially set for life. The future—for all of them—was bright with promise.

HIROSHI

7:00 a.m., Friday morning

Hiroshi sat at the breakfast table, quietly eating his eggs and toast. He had been grappling with a major question, but now, finally, he had reached a decision. He was going to sell his company—the one he had founded nearly ten years ago and had guided through thick and thin ever since—and start a new life chapter.

Hiroshi knew plenty of business owners who had exited their companies. Some of them had stayed on after, some hadn't. Some of them had sold to strategic buyers, some to private equity. Some of them had worked with dedicated sell-side advisors, others with full-scale investment banks. Some of them, like his friend Charles, had great outcomes, and some of them, like his friend Alma, did not. As he sat there, Hiroshi wondered what the "secret sauce" was. *Why* did some of them have great outcomes and others feel seller's remorse after they exited—or even worse, have a failed sale process?

Hiroshi knew that selling was the right decision, but he was afraid he would make a mistake and leave money on the table, or sell to someone who would dismantle his business or let his employees go. And really, his fear made sense: He knew he was a great leader for his own company, but he *wasn't* an expert at selling businesses.

As he sat at the breakfast table, Hiroshi wished he knew who to turn to for help. He wished he knew what steps he should take to ensure a successful exit. He knew he couldn't afford to make mistakes if he wanted to achieve his goals—for himself, his family, and his business. He wondered: *What do I do next?*

SELLING YOUR BUSINESS

Alma, Charles, and Hiroshi are fictional characters. But they represent real-life entrepreneurs who have found themselves in similar positions.

Selling a business is one of the most exciting—and hardest—things an entrepreneur or business owner will ever do. There are so many factors to consider and so many emotions to deal with. And no wonder: There's a *lot* on the line. Like Charles found, a well-planned and well-executed exit can create a financial windfall, give you a life of freedom, or even offer a way to scale your company to heights you might never otherwise achieve. But, like Alma discovered, a bad exit can have the opposite results. You might leave millions of dollars on the table, or set yourself and your company up for failure.

For all these reasons and more, selling your business, or even a portion of it, is an undertaking that no single person can guide you through. It's too big; there's too much at stake. That's why, in this book, you're going to hear from both of us—Andy Harris, a sell-side advisor to privately held businesses, and Jonathan Sherrill, an entrepreneur and business owner—as we take turns sharing our insights, experiences, and perspectives on the complex world of business exits. Between the two of us, we have almost six decades of experience starting, scaling, acquiring, and selling businesses.

Andy has worked as an M&A sell-side advisor for five years and has been involved with M&A for nineteen. In his capacity as a sell-side advisor, he's been involved with over one hundred transactions totaling in the billions of dollars to strategic and financial buyers. He's also served as the CEO for multiple manufacturing companies, during which time he acquired numerous companies. He's been on both sides of the table. He's seen what works and what doesn't.

Jonathan's experience is similarly robust. As an entrepreneur, he's been deeply involved with the successful sales of three businesses, so he knows exactly what it takes to get top valuation. Perhaps even more importantly, he knows how to maintain emotional fortitude while navigating the sometimes turbulent roller coaster of emotions that can come with the exit process.

Separately and together, we have been blessed to enjoy incredible success in our business and career ventures, and with this book, we are sharing the most important insights we've gleaned over the years with you. Whether you've just made the decision to sell (like Hiroshi) and are wondering what to do next, or you've sold a business before with less-than-optimal results (like Alma), our goal is to help you navigate the complexities of the sale process and wind up with an outcome like Charles had—and like what Jonathan achieved with Andy as his sell-side advisor.

We'll share the keys to a successful sale—no matter what your goals are—by covering the most important things you need to know. We'll demonstrate how a seasoned business coach can help you mentally prepare so that you can approach each decision with clarity and confidence. We'll discuss how to get clear on your *why* and examine why that clarity is such a fundamental part of achieving a successful outcome. And we'll look at what you need to know about hiring an elite sell-side advisor: someone who is an expert at running a strategic, competitive bid process, structuring the deal to protect your *must-haves*, and ultimately negotiating a deal far beyond what you thought was possible when you began.

But we won't stop there. We'll also explore ways to boost the value of your business in a buyer's eyes, from building a self-sustaining leadership team to being best prepared for the buyers' due diligence, to driving sales growth during the sale process.

Ultimately, by the time you're done reading this book, you'll know what steps to take next to secure your legacy and your future—and exit your business for maximum value and no regrets.

ANDY'S STORY
SEEKING A WIN-WIN EVERY TIME

When people hear the term *M&A advisor*—also known as a *sell-side advisor*, which is the term we will use in this book— they usually think of an investment banker. I get it. That's how the industry is usually framed. But I'm not an investment banker, and neither is anyone on my team. There's a reason I refer to myself as a *sell-side advisor*, and it's not just semantics. It's about how our firm and I work, the value we deliver, and the conflicts we avoid.

Traditional investment banks are full-service machines. They handle sell-side deals like we do, but they're also busy working buy-side transactions, raising debt, and even providing funding. Some have consulting arms or help companies go public. Sounds impressive, perhaps, but it creates a web of conflicting priorities. Imagine we're hired to sell a business, and one of the potential buyers is Microsoft. If we were a full-service bank, we might already be working with Microsoft on something else (e.g., helping them buy other companies or consulting on a project). Suddenly, we're stuck serving two masters.

If I'm working both sides of the table, I can't push Microsoft too hard for the seller. Sure, I might still close the deal and think, *Great, that was a win–win!* But that deal could've been worth double if I were advocating solely for the seller. That's the difference. That's why my team's *only* focus is getting the seller the absolute best deal, even if it means pushing the buyer to their limits. (In my experience, those limits make sense for the strategic value of the deal to the buyer, but are outside of the typical industry valuations set by a full-service investment bank.)

I've seen sellers leave tens or even hundreds of millions on the table because the advisors they trusted weren't fully in their corner. That doesn't happen with us. We're laser-focused on one thing: securing every penny the seller's business is worth.

WHY I DO WHAT I DO

My path to this role wasn't a straight line. I started as a chemical engineer at Exxon, the number one Fortune company in the world at the time, and a dream job for any young engineer. But after three years, I realized a technical career wasn't for me. I pivoted to technical sales and marketing, which turned out to be a crash course in business.

I worked across and served many industries—water treatment, chemicals, oil and gas, biotech, semiconductors, food and beverage, packaging, and personal care, to name just a few—learning what made businesses thrive and what made them stumble. Eventually, I moved into a leadership position, becoming VP of sales and marketing at a well-respected company where I learned to build teams, drive strategies, scale operations, and drive business growth.

In 2006, I achieved my ultimate goal when I became the CEO of a private equity–backed specialty chemicals company. Leading that company was transformative. I drove major growth, including leading an international acquisition spanning the US and Europe. When we sold the company in 2012, it wasn't one exit but three, unwinding the company with sales to three different strategic buyers for each of our unique business divisions—a complex process that taught me more about M&A than I ever imagined *and* sharpened my perspective about the buyer's viewpoint.

Following that experience, I became CEO of another private equity–backed specialty chemicals company. During my time there, I made fourteen strategic acquisitions in a five-year period, then sold the business to a strategic buyer. That was a truly Extraordinary Exit™: We provided investors 6.5x their invested equity.

It was from my time leading these two companies that I began to really understand the power of doing a "buy-and-build" acquisitive roll-up with a focus on an ultimate exit.

The experience of these strategic acquisitions, integrations, and significant exits changed my life. Afterward, I decided to use everything I'd learned about leadership, strategy, building businesses, and selling businesses to help other owners—like you—navigate the daunting process of selling their companies. I've been in your shoes. I know what it's like to pour your life into building something and risk being shortchanged at the end. I also know what it's like to be in the buyer's shoes, seeking acquisitions that create strategic value. That's why I do this—not just to get deals done, but to get the *right* deals done. When a seller hires me and our firm, they know I'm 100 percent in their corner, with no distractions and no conflicts. There's just a relentless focus on securing the best possible outcome.

My background gave me a front-row seat to the mechanics of financial/private equity and strategic acquisitions. As a "hired gun" CEO, I navigated more than twenty acquisitions (ranging from tens of millions to hundreds of millions of dollars), handled international roll-ups, orchestrated integrations that brought out the best in both parties, and led six strategic exits. By 2020, when I met Rob Follows, the founder of STS, I was ready for a new challenge: helping business owners maximize the value of their businesses while achieving their personal and professional goals, and at the same time bringing greater purpose to the second half of my life.

Rob's pitch was compelling: *Instead of building businesses for private equity, why don't you help families and entrepreneurs who've built businesses sell to strategics for maximum value and optimal personal outcomes? Help them ensure the legacy that they've devoted their lives to will thrive.* When I heard that, it was a no-brainer. While the private equity model typically is to buy low and sell high, strategics often pay significant premiums—anywhere from 30 to 300 percent more, in fact—when the fit is right.

The goal in selling a business isn't just to cash out, but to create something transformational. The right deal doesn't just preserve your legacy; it amplifies it, unlocking new potential for both parties. Take a recent deal we did as an example. A small medical device parts manufacturer specialized in automated, rapid prototyping, which requires nimble, high-precision work to quickly develop and produce parts for FDA approval. Once the part was approved, the manufacturer had the capacity to produce up to one million of those parts per year. If demand exceeded that threshold, though, production got moved to a larger-volume contract manufacturer. Their strategic buyer was an automotive parts manufacturer with huge manufacturing capacity (they can accommodate manufacturing up to one hundred million parts per year) but no capability for this type of work. At first, it seemed like an odd pairing, but strategically, it was genius. The buyer diversified into the steady medical device market while simultaneously gaining the ability to provide rapid prototyping "innovation" capabilities to their automotive clients, while the seller gained resources to scale production to high volumes for growing clients. Both companies emerged stronger, proving that the right deal isn't just one plus one—it's far more.

THE IMPORTANCE OF PREPARATION

A common misconception among business owners is that selling to a strategic buyer means losing control or watching your business get gutted. Many fear, *If I sell to a strategic buyer, they'll shut down my plant/business location and lay off my team.* Yes, that's a risk with the wrong buyer, so the key is to find a strategic buyer who sees your business as a vital asset for their growth. They desperately need your location(s), teams, technology, manufacturing capabilities, sales channels, customers, and all the other unique elements that can give them a greater competitive advantage.

Bottom line: When both parties realize transformative gains, it's the holy grail of a strategic transaction.

A perfect example of this can be found in one deal I handled recently. The buyer needed additional capacity to meet growing demand and saw the seller's business as the perfect solution. They retained the original site, leveraged its expertise, and scaled operations—all while preserving and even *increasing* jobs. Strategic buyers often focus on your business's transformative potential, which is why they're willing to pay a premium.

But here's the thing: The best deals aren't just about luck—they're about preparation.

Positioning your business as an irresistible opportunity often requires groundwork. Another client, for example, had worked with a coach to refine operations and build a stronger team. By the time we got involved, their business was already primed to attract top buyers. Coaching isn't mandatory but can be transformative. Coaches help address strategy, operations, and leadership gaps, which can boost value significantly. A good example is a client who sold direct-to-consumer online. They pivoted to an omni-channel strategy, and as a result, they landed major retailers like Home Depot and Lowe's. That shift added to their brand and increased both buyer interest and valuation.

Ultimately, the best deals benefit both sides. The buyer gains a critical asset and a competitive advantage, and the seller maximizes the value of their hard work while securing their team's future. That's why I say selling a business isn't just about the numbers; it's about finding the right fit and unlocking potential to transform both your business and your life.

JONATHAN

THE LIFE-CHANGING EXPERIENCE OF A BUSINESS SALE

Selling a business you've invested so much into is a life-changing experience. For anyone who's built a business from the ground up, you know it's not just about numbers on a balance sheet. It's years of effort, relationships, and sacrifice. I know, because *I've been there*—not once, but multiple times.

My business journey began at age fourteen, working in my dad and uncle's metal roofing manufacturing business. This wasn't a cushy family job. I did everything from cutting materials and sweeping floors to folding steel and managing deliveries. It was scrappy, hard work that taught me the value of every role in a company.

As the business grew, so did I. I moved into operations, then sales, and eventually became general manager, overseeing fifty employees by the time my dad and uncle sold the company to a family office–backed private equity firm in 2010. That sale introduced me to the world of M&A and gave me a crash course in business finance. Around the same time, I was taking college business classes, applying what I learned in real time during due diligence. It was at once exhausting and invigorating.

After the sale, I became COO and eventually president, leading the business to expand from one location to five across Florida. It was a period of profound change for me, as I shifted from an entrepreneurial mindset to leading like a professional executive. I built a leadership team, implemented structured systems, and embraced the strategic side of growth.

During that time, I fell in love with the professional side of business. Scaling through systems, operations, human capital, board meetings, and strategic growth projections was a far cry from the "do-it-all-yourself" approach I'd grown up with. And while we focused on organic growth, I became fascinated with acquisitions and roll-ups, devouring everything I could about private equity and M&A. That curiosity would shape the next phase of my career.

BEYOND THE CROSSROADS

In 2017, I hit a crossroads. After twenty-five years with the company, I approached the owner about becoming an equity partner. My first conversation went well, but a few months later, he gave me a clear answer: *No*. The company wasn't structured for partners, and he didn't see it happening. I pressed again, but in February 2017, the owner said, "It's clear you want to be an entrepreneur, and there's no room for that here."

Just like that, I was out. After two decades of dedication, I was escorted out the side door, without even a chance to say goodbye to the team I'd built. It was gut-wrenching.

As painful as it was, that moment turned out to be a blessing. It freed me to eventually start my own business—one that, as you'll see throughout this book, I eventually exited with a strategic deal that far exceeded my initial expectations.

Every business sale is deeply personal. For the seller, it's the culmination of years or even decades of hard work, long hours, and personal sacrifice. That's why it's about more than getting a good deal. It's about finding the right buyer to carry your vision forward and care for the people who built it.

So, like I said, I've been in your shoes. I know what it's like to dedicate everything to a business and face the uncertainty of what comes next. That's why I wanted to write this book: to help you get maximum value (like I did) while ensuring your business finds the right home and you achieve all of your desired personal outcomes. Selling isn't the end. On the contrary, it's a chance to see your vision soar.

THE BEGINNING OF QUICKEN STEEL

Starting a business isn't always a tidy or straightforward process. Often, it's messy, unpredictable, and shaped by challenges you won't see coming. My journey began with lessons I didn't realize I'd need: working in my dad's metal roofing business, going through its sale, and eventually getting fired from the very company I helped grow.

After my departure, I was at a loss. With a six-month severance package, a noncompete agreement that encompassed the entire southeastern US, and a family to support, I started exploring options. Moving to Colorado and starting a metal roofing company seemed promising—it got me out of the territory covered by the noncompete, and it let me build a business in the industry I knew so well. But when we went to Colorado to scout it out, my wife, Dana, got severe altitude sickness. Back in Florida, my dad suggested I join him in growing Quicken Manufacturing, a small building manufacturing operation he had started. I was hesitant at first, but when he mentioned the cutting-edge manufacturing equipment on order, I saw an opportunity to build something new. I agreed to join him.

The main challenge we faced was finding manufacturing space. Those 150-foot-long machines needed a very large facility. My dad found an old Georgia-Pacific sawmill in Cross City, Florida, and planned some renovations. Then fate intervened. While selling off the old sawmill equipment, my dad met some people in the industry who wanted to restart the mill. That plan took off, they bought the sawmill equipment and the property, and soon Georgia-Pacific offered him another opportunity in Claxton, Georgia, a town better known for its fruitcake than its business prospects.

Despite the unknowns, we sold Quicken Manufacturing— an undertaking that I spearheaded—and moved to Claxton to start fresh. That's when Quicken Steel was born, with my dad and me as partners. It wasn't easy. Dana had to shut down her successful children's boutique in Florida and move to a place neither of us had ever heard of, and my non-solicit agreement meant I could bring only one employee, Cody, with me (fortunately, Cody was a jack-of-all-trades).

The sixty-acre property and fifty thousand square feet of buildings were in rough shape, but I was driven by a clear vision: to build a business rooted in innovation and efficiency.

Renovating the facility proved a monumental task. The floors were uneven, the roofs leaked, and my office felt like it was stuck in the 1960s. Yet, standing in that run-down office,

I felt a long-lost excitement. Starting from scratch was humbling but energizing. It forced us to be resourceful and solve problems on the fly. Quicken Steel was the culmination of everything I'd learned, from running a family business to navigating a corporate sale. It wasn't the path I'd envisioned, but as I stood in that old sawmill office surrounded by possibility, I knew I was exactly where I was meant to be.

START WITH THE END IN MIND

From day one, I made a decision that shaped every move we made: Start with the end in mind. I was strategically building the business for an exit, so we built scalability, efficiency, and long-term value into every process, purchase, and decision.

I'd learned the hard way about the importance of starting with the right systems. For example, in the previous business, we relied on QuickBooks to manage the business and accounting, which worked until the new owners demanded an enterprise resource planning (ERP) system. If you've ever implemented an ERP system at a company that's already up and running, you know it's like open-heart surgery for a business. At Quicken Steel, we skipped that chaos by investing in a robust ERP system from the very beginning. Even when it was just me running the show, I thought big—envisioning seamless digital workflows that would scale with the company.

My dad and I were co-founders, but he left the day-to-day leadership to me. That was fine. I was ready to roll up my sleeves. Our initial plan was simple. We would manufacture specialty steel building components and, once my noncompete expired, reenter the metal roofing market. But we quickly realized the Georgia roofing market wasn't like Florida's. Residential demand was weaker, and our model didn't fit. So, we pivoted to self-storage, selling components and complete engineered building packages all across the country.

As we grew, we shifted from direct building sales to building dealer networks, which allowed us to scale without handling every transaction ourselves. These pivots—first to self-storage, then to dealers—were game-changers. If we'd clung to our original plan, we'd have missed out on massive opportunities.

While we were focused on what we ultimately wanted to achieve, we didn't try to stick to a rigid script. Instead, we stayed flexible while keeping an eye on the bigger picture. This approach made Quicken Steel not only more successful, but also more attractive to buyers. By the time we sold in 2022, we'd built a scalable, diversified business primed for growth. Those early decisions to think long-term, embrace flexibility, and build for scalability laid the foundation for everything that followed. And when it came time to sell, they made all the difference.

COACHING MATTERS

Being coached wasn't something I actively sought out. It found me unexpectedly but became one of the most meaningful parts of my entrepreneurial journey. It taught me the value of having someone in your corner and the importance of adapting the relationship to fit your needs.

It was March 2021, about three and a half years into Quicken Steel. We were growing fast, and I was hiring to build out the leadership team. I posted an ad for a salesperson and was surprised when a retired Apache helicopter pilot/Army Ranger applied. During the interviews, I realized his skills were better suited for operations (which was a role we desperately needed to fill anyway), so I hired him with the potential to promote him to operations manager. However, I wasn't sure how to transition someone with such a strong military background into a civilian manufacturing role. Seeking advice, I posted in a YPO (Young Presidents' Organization) network and was connected to a coach from CEO Coaching International. That first call made a huge impact on me. As a seasoned, successful CEO himself, the coach didn't just offer hiring advice. He helped me think more strategically about leadership and business challenges. By the end of the call, he suggested exploring coaching further. Skeptical but curious, I decided to give it a try.

At first, we had biweekly sessions, but the cadence felt off. I was running a high-growth, fast-paced manufacturing business: Too much happened between calls, and we spent most of the time catching up instead of solving real-time issues. Frustrated, I told him, "This isn't working." Instead

of pushing back, he adjusted. We switched to weekly, shorter calls and dropped the pre-call homework. It was a simple change, but it made it all click. Suddenly, coaching became an integral part of my decision-making, helping me tackle challenges and uncover opportunities in real time.

Just a few months later, I was preparing to sell the business, and my coach was with me every step of the way, offering invaluable support during one of the most intense periods of my career. Looking back, the timing felt like divine intervention.

Some entrepreneurs question the value of coaching. They think, *Why pay someone to tell me what I can figure out myself?* But even the best athletes rely on specialized coaches to refine their performance, and business is no different. A good coach doesn't do the work for you. They challenge, guide, and hold you accountable, and they bring fresh perspectives and strategic thinking. The key is to find someone whose style aligns with your needs. A great coach pushes you without overwhelming you, adapting to your goals and priorities. If that isn't your experience with one coach, move on to another until you find the right fit.

For me, coaching was hugely meaningful, especially during the lead-up to selling Quicken Steel. My coach helped me make critical decisions and stay focused on my vision and values. He provided clarity and alignment when I needed it most.

Coaching taught me that having someone in your corner isn't a weakness. It's a tool for growth. Remember, selling a business isn't just about closing a deal. It's about maximizing value, finding the right buyer, and ensuring that the legacy you've built will thrive. That's why Andy and I are here: We're the coaches in your corner. Through our collective experience, we can help you achieve outcomes that reflect your hard work and dedication, leaving nothing on the table and no regrets.

Sounds good, right? That's why, in the upcoming chapters, we're going to give you a crash course in what it takes to maximize value and get the most out of selling your business. We'll also explore key takeaways that Hiroshi (and you) can use to help ensure success. Let's get started.

THE DECISION TO SELL

JONATHAN

THE DECISION TO SELL MY BUSINESS WAS deeply personal. From the day I started the company, I knew I would sell it eventually. My original plan was to build it over fifteen or twenty years before considering an exit. But life had other plans. When my daughter Faith turned two, she was diagnosed with autism. Running a rapidly growing company while managing my personal responsibilities with my family became overwhelming. By the time my daughter turned twelve, I realized that selling the business would not only provide financial security but, more importantly, create the flexibility to focus on my family.

The combination of managing rapid business growth and navigating these challenges was intense. The struggle to

43

balance everything reinforced my desire to move on—and to create lifelong financial security for my family, especially my daughter.

At the time, the business was scaling fast. In fact, in the twelve months following our decision to sell, our revenue more than doubled. Growth like that brings its own kind of stress. You're constantly making decisions, solving problems, and trying to keep the momentum going. With everything going on, the pressure began to intensify.

The real turning point came during a family vacation to Maine. We'd taken a week to visit Dana's family and spend some time off the grid. Maine in the summer is beautiful—coastal views, lobster dinners, and time to unwind. We stayed in a primitive cabin in the small town of Patten, surrounded by nature. It was exactly what I needed to clear my head.

One evening, as the vacation was winding down, I went for a walk. I've always found solace in nature. Throughout my life, I've realized that getting outside and walking allows me to get quiet and listen to God, and that day was no exception. It was getting dark, and I found myself alone with my thoughts, praying about the business and the issues that waited for me there. And then something happened that I'll never forget.

I had what I can only describe as an open vision. In the dark, I saw a dim amber light hovering over a book—a Bible. The light guided me to a specific passage: Isaiah 58:6–7. I pulled out my phone and opened my Bible app to read the passage and was struck by the words: *"Is not this the kind of fasting I have chosen: to loose the chains of injustice and untie the cords of the yoke, to set the oppressed free? Is it not to share your food with the hungry and to provide the poor wanderer with shelter—when you see the naked, to clothe them, and not to turn away from your own flesh and blood?"*

It was a powerful moment, and while it didn't immediately lead to the decision to sell, it planted a seed. As I reflected on the verse, I realized that my "flesh and blood" was my daughter, and it was up to me to prioritize her well-being and do everything I possibly could to set her up for success in every area of her life. As we drove the twenty-four hours back to Georgia, that experience stayed with me.

A few days later, as I was sitting in my living room preparing to return to work, the thought hit me: *Maybe it's time to sell the business.* It wasn't something I'd actively been considering, but the idea gave me an immediate sense of peace.

I mentioned it to Dana, and while she was understandably hesitant, worried about what life would look like post-sale, she listened to what I had to say with an open mind and an open heart. Then I called my dad, who was also my financial partner, expecting him to push back. To my surprise, he supported the idea, telling me, "If that's what you want to do, I'm good with it." That validation gave me the confidence to explore the idea further.

Throughout the process, Faith was both my anchor and my focus. Remember, she was diagnosed with autism at two years old. At the time, she was twelve, and I felt deeply that the next five years would be critical for her development. I wanted to be there for her in ways I couldn't be while running a fast-growing business.

I also thought about her future. I didn't know what adulthood would look like for her, but I wanted to make sure she would be financially secure no matter what. A verse, Proverbs 13:22, kept coming to mind: *"A good man leaves an inheritance for his children's children."* That became my guiding principle. I wasn't just selling the business for financial freedom. I was doing it because I wanted to be there for Faith in every part of her life and to give her the best opportunity to succeed, whatever that looked like for her.

Once the decision was made, I brought the idea to my coach, John. His guidance was instrumental in helping me navigate the next steps. He also introduced me to my M&A sell-side advisor—and now co-author—Andy, who helped me see and realize the potential value of the business.

When I first ran the numbers, based on my previous experience with multiples of EBITDA (earnings before interest, taxes, depreciation, and amortization), I had modest expectations for the business's valuation. But over the next year, as we moved through the sale process, the business continued to grow, and the valuation kept climbing. Andy's insights, experience as a prior CEO, and M&A expertise showed me that the business could sell strategically for significantly more than I'd initially thought. By the time we closed the sale, the final number was more than three times what I'd anticipated when I first considered selling just twelve months earlier.

FIND YOUR WHY

Selling a business is an emotional and personal journey. I knew why I wanted to do it. I wanted to create a future where I could focus on what mattered most: my family.

If you're considering selling your business, my advice is to start with your *why*. Andy gave me this advice when I started working with him, and I quickly realized those are words to live by. Whether it's family, financial freedom, or a new chapter in life, understanding your purpose will keep you grounded through the highs and lows of the process.

Beyond that, remember that it's never too early to prepare. Build systems, document processes, and surround yourself with the right people. That way, when the time comes, you'll be ready to make the leap with confidence and clarity.

When you're running a business, especially one in high-growth mode, the decisions you make can feel monumental. Deciding to sell will only compound that feeling. It demands a deep connection to your *why*. Without it, the obstacles and doubts along the way can derail you. There will be moments when you'll question everything. *Why am I doing this? Is it worth the stress? Am I making the right choice?* For me, having my *why* written down and anchored to something bigger than myself kept me on track during those moments.

Not everyone's *why* will be the same as mine. Maybe yours is about financial freedom, finding the right partner to help scale the business, starting a new business, or simply stepping back to enjoy life. Whatever it is, you have to find it, and it has to be strong enough to carry you through the tough days that will inevitably come.

If you're struggling to find your *why*, take the time you need to get crystal clear on it. For me, as you know, that clarity came during a week in nature, away from the distractions and stress of daily life. Whether it's taking a weekend alone, going on a fishing trip, or playing a quiet round of golf, find what works for you. Disconnect, reflect, and give yourself the space to hear that inner voice. And if you're struggling to uncover your purpose, don't be afraid to ask for help. Talk to your spouse, your coach, or a trusted advisor.

One tool that can be helpful is the Seven Levels of Why, which was adapted from an exercise developed by Sakichi Toyoda, the founder of Toyota Industries. Here's how it works: Start with a specific statement or goal, such as "I want to sell my business." Then, ask yourself, "Why?" The answer becomes the basis for the next "Why?" and so on. By the

THE DECISION TO SELL

seventh iteration, the responses often reveal deeper personal values, motivations, or root causes.

For example:

- Why do I want to sell my business? "Because I want financial freedom."
- Why do I want financial freedom? "Because I want to be able to spend more time with my family."
- Why do I want to spend more time with my family? "Because I have a special-needs daughter, and I want to make sure she has everything she needs to succeed in life."
- And so on...

This process is designed to go beyond initial, often superficial answers to identify the real emotional drivers behind your decision.

There's a power in understanding that there's a *why* behind people's actions. Whether it's a rude waiter, an overzealous diligence request during an acquisition, or a frustrating employee, I've found that taking a moment to remember that the other person is driven by an underlying *why* driving their actions—even if I don't know what that *why* is—can completely change how I respond to them and the situation. And you can do the same thing for yourself. Uncover the real core motivation behind your desire to sell. This will give you clarity amid the chaos.

Pro tip here: One of the most valuable things I did during this process was take the time to put my *why* in writing—and then refer to it constantly. I suggest you do the same; it will help you align the sale with your values and priorities. I wrote down everything: my financial goals, the scriptures that guided me, and the reasons behind my decision. This practice helped me stay focused and avoid getting lost in the chaos of the sale.

I can't recommend this step highly enough. Write down your *why* and be specific. Then make sure every decision aligns with your ultimate goals. Refer back to it as the offers start to come in.

BALANCE ACTION WITH TRUST

As someone who has been through the sales of multiple businesses, I can tell you beyond a shadow of a doubt that selling a business is emotionally taxing. You're balancing personal stress, family considerations, and the enormous responsibility of growing the company while simultaneously preparing it for sale. It's easy to feel overwhelmed, and I wasn't immune to that.

One of the most impactful books I read during this time was *The Surrender Experiment* by Michael A. Singer. His philosophy of serving the moment in front of you resonated deeply with me. The idea is to focus on what's within your control,

THE DECISION TO SELL

do it with excellence, and trust that the rest will unfold as it should. The point is not to take your foot off the gas but, instead, to let go of the need to control every outcome.

For example, when I had to choose an M&A advisor, I didn't obsess over finding the "perfect" one. I trusted the process, leaned into recommendations from my coach, and chose Andy because everything about his approach aligned with what I needed. That trust, as you'll see, paid off in ways I couldn't have predicted.

Another book that shaped my mindset was James Allen's *The Way of Peace*, which taught me to recognize and release selfish tendencies, both in myself and in others. When I felt stress creeping in, I could step back, almost humorously, and observe myself getting worked up. It was a way to keep my emotions in check and focus on what really mattered.

Faith also played a significant role in grounding me. The Bible verse *"Cast all your cares on the Lord"* (1 Peter 5:7) was a constant reminder that I didn't have to carry the weight of everything on my own. Combining that foundation with the insights from Singer and Allen gave me a balanced perspective that allowed me to stay focused, productive, and relatively calm throughout the process.

Avoiding stress altogether is impossible, especially when you're selling your business. Instead, aim to develop tools and practices that help you navigate stress effectively. For me, that included prayer, long walks in nature, talking with my coach and Andy, and simply taking the time to disconnect and reset. When you're in the thick of due diligence or dealing with a challenging negotiation, having built-in tools that will keep you calm is invaluable.

DON'T WAIT FOR THE "PERFECT" TIME

Knowing *when* to sell is one of the toughest challenges for entrepreneurs. The perfect time can feel elusive. For me, the decision didn't come from market trends or data but from that moment of clarity in Maine. I realized I couldn't control external factors like the economy or political conditions, and fixating on them only added stress. Instead, I focused on the present, often finding stillness through walking or prayer.

Trying to time everything perfectly would've been impossible. A year before the sale, our growth was impressive, but what followed was extraordinary. Our size and profits more than doubled, exceeding all expectations. After the deal closed, the market sharply declined, and margins like ours likely wouldn't have been possible. In hindsight, the timing was perfect, though I didn't fully see it then. As the deal approached, I felt a sense of urgency, but I now realize that stress wasn't necessary. God had it under control. Trusting in Him gave me the strength to let go of the need to control every outcome.

DEVELOP EMOTIONAL RESILIENCE

I've actually been through three business sales over the course of my career. The first sale happened in 2010, and looking back, I see it as a trial by fire. I prayed, of course, but I didn't yet understand how to truly let go and trust the process. It was a grind that left me drained. The sale of Quicken Steel in 2022 was different. I still worked hard and showed up for what needed to be done, but I didn't let fear or frustration dictate my actions.

Selling a business is as much about emotional resilience as it is about financial strategy, planning, and trusting the process. By focusing on what you can control, letting go of what you can't, and staying anchored to your purpose, you'll not only survive the process; you'll come out stronger on the other side.

HIROSHI

Sitting in his office, Hiroshi hung up the phone and clenched his jaw, deep in thought. His friend Alma had just closed on her business, but when he called to congratulate her, she didn't sound as happy as he had expected. Instead, she sounded like she had a lot of regrets. It shook him; he had made the decision to sell, and the last thing he wanted to do was leave money on the table or end up with seller's remorse.

When he asked her about it, Alma told him she wished she had gotten clearer on her *why*, right from the beginning. That would have made the arduous sale process much easier, she said, and helped her figure out *exactly* what she needed to get from the sale to achieve her goals.

The more they talked, the more convinced Hiroshi became that finding his *why* was crucial, too—and that there was no time like the present to do so. As soon as they hung up, he grabbed a notepad and a pen and, using a technique called the Seven Levels of Why he had recently read about, he began brainstorming.

CLARITY, ALIGNMENT, AND THE EMOTIONAL JOURNEY

ANDY

ELLING A BUSINESS IS MORE THAN JUST A financial transaction—it's a *life* transition. Getting clarity on your motivation and required outcomes can mean the difference between a successful exit and a regret-filled decision. The Seven Levels of Why is one great way to start to explore that. Another exercise—one that our firm and I guide each client through when we start working with them—can help you define **two more key points:**

1. **Required Outcomes**: *Things that absolutely must happen for the sale to be worthwhile*
2. **Preferred Outcomes**: *Nice-to-have benefits, but not deal-breakers*

Before diving into financials or valuations, we walk sellers through the exercise I mentioned at the beginning of the chapter, to help them define their goals. We ask thought-provoking and necessary questions, including:

- Why are you selling?
- What does life look like after the sale?
- What are the required outcomes that must be met for this to be a success?
- What are the preferred but flexible outcomes?
- If multiple owners or family members are involved, are you aligned?

These conversations happen *before* calling potential buyers. If alignment isn't there from the start, it can derail deals at the worst possible moment, often when emotions are running high.

Even if a deal isn't at risk of going south, answering these questions can still mean the difference between a disappointing outcome like Alma's and a favorable one like Charles's. For example, imagine a scenario where a high-valuation offer comes in, but it doesn't meet one of the seller's *must-haves*—like ensuring the business remains intact rather than being absorbed and dismantled. This sort of situation happens all the time, and having these priorities documented helps everyone stay on the same page. Sellers can revisit their original purpose and align their decisions with what truly matters, even if it means making trade-offs, like accepting a slightly lower valuation to secure a buyer who will respect their legacy and care for their employees.

Many owners begin the sale process thinking, *I'm tired of running the business—I'm ready to be done.* But what does *done* actually look like? What happens the day after the sale closes? For some, like my co-author, Jonathan, the goal is to walk away completely. For others, it's about taking some chips off the table while still remaining involved in a reduced capacity. Either way, getting clear on expectations *and* what you must have to achieve those goals is crucial not just for the seller, but for potential buyers as well.

BEWARE THE "MISALIGNMENT TRAP"

One of the biggest obstacles to a smooth sale is misalignment, whether that's between business partners or family members, or even within the seller's own expectations. Some business owners believe they want to sell, but they *are* the business. The operations, strategy, and customer relationships are so dependent on them that a clean break can make it nearly impossible for the buyer to continue successfully. We call that *founder risk*, because the business is too dependent on the founder or the leader. In cases like these, the seller may need to take time to put a successor in place, or build a management team that can run the business without them. A buyer won't pay top dollar for a company that may fall apart the moment the owner steps away.

Alignment is also important when multiple stakeholders are involved. If there are other shareholders or partners, their *why* needs to be understood as well. Selling a business isn't a solo decision. It requires everyone involved to ensure a smooth transition.

AVOID UNNECESSARY DERAILMENT

Even when a seller has a clear *why* at the beginning, emotions can throw everything off course. Case in point: One of our clients had a multigenerational business. The second generation—the daughter of the founder—had been appointed president and had been providing daily leadership for the past five years, while the founders were preparing to retire. The original owners had been clear from the start that they were ready to move into their golden years, travel, and focus on philanthropy. Their daughter wanted to stay and grow the company with a new partner, and everything was moving toward a successful exit.

But as the closing date approached, the father started having second thoughts. He began questioning what he would do without the business. He even insisted on keeping his full salary post-sale as an advisor to the new owner and board, despite the fact that the buyer no longer needed him in the CEO role. Suddenly, what had been a clear exit plan became clouded by doubt and uncertainty.

It took a joint meeting with the father and his wife to realign everything. She reminded him of their original decision to sell the business and enjoy this next stage of life together. That moment of clarity was all he needed. The deal moved forward, and they successfully transitioned into their new chapter.

This kind of thing happens more often than people realize. Selling a business is a deeply personal process, and even the most rational business owner can find themselves second-guessing the decision. The most well-planned exits can be derailed by unexpected doubts. That's why it's so important to document and align your *why* early in the process, because when emotions take over, you need an anchor to ride out the storm.

WATCH OUT FOR TIMING PITFALLS

There's no single right answer for when to sell, but there are some red flags that signal a seller might not be ready. If someone's only motivation is getting the highest possible valuation, for example, that can be a risky foundation. Maximizing value is always a goal, but if that's the only consideration, other important factors like family wealth planning, legacy, spiritual alignment, and/or employee well-being can get overlooked. The most successful exits are well-rounded decisions, not just financial ones.

Another common reason for selling is one of the "*Six Ds*"— *Death*, *Disenchantment*, *Divorce*, *Disability*, *Distress*, or *Disagreement*. While these are all legitimate reasons, they can create a sense of urgency for the seller that leads to poor decisions. In these situations, my team and I encourage sellers to pause, step back, and manage the timeline strategically rather than rushing into a fire sale. Even in difficult circumstances, taking time to run a competitive process will result in a better outcome—one that can be two to three times what the seller would otherwise have realized.

This is just one reason why it's smart to have a good advisor—specifically, an exclusively sell-side advisor—on your side. They will act as a guide and reality check throughout the process, helping you navigate one of the most significant transitions of your life. They'll ask the right questions, help realign expectations, and make sure you don't lose sight of your original goals. There's another benefit beyond these as well: While sell-side advisors aren't therapists, the best ones have been in your position many times before and provide a human touch that can help you manage the mix of excitement, fear, and uncertainty that comes with letting go.

CLARITY, ALIGNMENT, AND THE EMOTIONAL JOURNEY

TAKE THE MOST IMPORTANT STEP

Jonathan's experience selling his business is a perfect case study on the value of finding your *why*, and why defining your *must-haves* (i.e., your required outcomes) and *nice-to-haves* (i.e., preferred outcomes) up front is so critical.

Ultimately, Jonathan was presented with two compelling offers: one from a private equity group, and a slightly lower offer from a privately held, strategic buyer. He chose the latter, as he knew private equity firms don't buy businesses to keep them. The strategic buyer had long-term plans to invest in the business, grow it, and even expand it nationally. Jonathan also believed this buyer would take care of his hardworking employees and give the company a strong future.

If Jonathan hadn't clearly documented his priorities at the beginning, he might have been tempted to go with the highest number on the table. It's easy to be swayed by extra dollars when the offers are staring you in the face. But when he came back to his *why*, the decision became clear.

Just like their *whys*, every entrepreneur's *must-haves* are different. Some want to stay involved in the business post-sale, while others want a clean break. The key is for the advisor to focus on customization—tailoring the process to fit the seller's unique situation and ensuring their priorities remain front and center.

REMEMBER: NOT EVERY HIGH OFFER IS A GOOD OFFER

Beyond the emotional aspect, sellers also need to define their *why* and their *must-haves* (and *nice-to-haves*) when considering the practical side of how a deal is structured. Many sellers make the mistake of focusing only on the total price without thinking about how and when they actually get paid. For example, let's say you receive two offers:

- **Offer 1:** $180 million, all cash at closing
- **Offer 2:** $170 million up front, plus a $10 million earnout after one year and another $10 million earnout after two years

At first glance, Offer 2 looks better—it totals $190 million—but here's the thing: Earnouts are *not guaranteed*. They typically depend on the business hitting specific revenue or profit targets after the sale. If the seller's goal was to fully exit the business, taking the second offer might mean staying involved longer just to ensure those extra payments come through. If the buyer makes changes, restructures operations, or shifts strategy, those targets might not be hit, and the seller might never see that extra $20 million.

For business owners with family members or other shareholders involved, alignment is even more important. My team and I always make it a point to meet all key stakeholders early in the process, whether that's co-owners, spouses, or the next generation. If there are differences in expectations, those need to be addressed *before* we begin the process and go to market.

In one particular case, a second-generation sibling team fully owned and ran a business they were preparing to sell. One of them had an adult child working in the company who loved the business but didn't want to be an owner. They wanted to stay in a leadership role but had no desire to take over entirely. That distinction was critical in finding the right buyer. The second-generation owners wanted to exit completely, but the third-generation family member wanted to stay involved. The right buyer had to be willing to support both outcomes—purchasing the company while also retaining key talent.

In the end, we were able to find them a perfect fit. The second-generation owners were able to fully exit in the first year, and the third-generation family member moved into a head of sales VP role for the newly combined company. It was a great win–win, but it happened only because the family had honest conversations with us up front about their individual goals so we could find a deal that was structured to meet all of their needs *and* achieve a maximum valuation due to the integrated strategic value with the buyer.

These examples demonstrate why getting clear on your *why*, your *must-haves*, and your *nice-to-haves*—and communicating those points to your advisor—is so important. Ultimately, they're the foundation to making sure the final deal structure aligns with your goals.

HIROSHI, CHARLES, AND ALMA

Hiroshi walked into the restaurant, scanning the room for his friends. Seeing Charles and Alma at a table, he hurried over. Standing, they both hugged him, then everyone took their seats. "So glad you could join us, Hiroshi," Charles said, beaming at him.

Smiling, Hiroshi nodded. "I'm so excited to treat you both to lunch! I know you both completed your sale processes last month; I want to celebrate with you!"

Alma smiled at that, but her eyes looked a little strained. "Still feeling some regret about how everything went, Alma?" Hiroshi asked.

Looking down, she nodded her head. "It wasn't the worst outcome, I guess," she said. "But there are a lot of things I wish I had done differently."

"I know we talked about how important it is to find your *why* before you even list the business," Hiroshi said. "But what else do you think I should know? I'm hoping to start the process soon, so any advice you have would be much appreciated."

"For me, hiring a dedicated sell-side advisor made a huge difference," Charles said. Nodding, Alma replied,

"Yeah, I didn't have a dedicated advisor, and it was a mistake."

"Why?" asked Hiroshi.

"Well, for one—and this is just one example—they helped me see that the offer that looked highest on paper wasn't necessarily the best offer," Charles responded. "When we looked at the highest offer, we saw that it had earnouts and other conditions that would have interfered with my *why*—traveling the world with my family. I wanted to be completely done with the business, and those conditions would have tied me to it. Having someone I trusted in my corner to help me see that made it easier to pick an offer that got me everything I wanted."

"That would have been really helpful," Alma said. "Honestly, the process dragged on, and a lot of times I felt kind of alone. Having someone looking out for my specific interests—someone who was experienced and could walk me through every step of the process *and* help me figure out what I needed to do to achieve the best possible outcome—would have been invaluable."

That makes sense, Hiroshi thought. *When I get back to the office, I should look into what I need to know about hiring a dedicated sell-side advisor.*

SELECTING THE RIGHT SELL-SIDE ADVISOR

ANDY

OMETIMES, BUSINESS OWNERS START THINK-
ing about selling because buyers are already knocking
on their door. A private equity firm or strategic buyer
expresses interest, and suddenly the seller realizes they
could get a significant offer for their business. It's tempting to think, *I don't need an advisor—I already have a buyer, and
they've floated a price I would take.* But more often than not,
that mindset leaves significant dollars on the table. Perhaps
more importantly, deals like this often fall apart because the
seller is unprepared for the complexity of negotiations, difficult discussions with the buyer, and the emotional roller
coaster that comes with getting the deal closed.

Many assume selling is simply a matter of agreeing on a price. The reality is, price is just one of many factors in a deal. Once an offer is made, negotiations shift to deal structure, working capital adjustments, indemnifications, holdbacks, employment agreements, transition service agreements, and numerous other terms that can dramatically impact the final outcome. Without an advisor managing these details, sellers can find themselves overwhelmed, leading to unnecessary concessions, conflicts, and—in many cases—failed deals.

You can think of a sell-side advisor like a great sports coach. Take Michael Jordan and Phil Jackson, for example. Jordan was the one out on the court, making the plays and sinking the shots. There's no question that he was a master of his craft. But Jordan knew he couldn't do it alone. He needed someone to help him perfect his strategy, his execution, and his mindset. Phil Jackson was that someone. Jackson was so important to Michael Jordan's success, in fact, that Jordan said he wouldn't work with any other coach. When it comes to your business, *you* are Michael Jordan—the master of your craft. But to enjoy the greatest success possible when selling, you need to find the advisor equivalent of Phil Jackson.

MAKE YOUR ADVISOR YOUR TRUSTED PARTNER

On average, the process of selling a business takes nine months or more, and it is often an emotional roller coaster.

Entrusting this process to someone who truly understands its significance is critically important, which is why choosing the right sell-side advisor matters so much. You need a trusted partner who aligns with your vision, operates with integrity, personally knows what it's like to lead a business (not to mention prepare it for sale and then sell it), and will make your exit journey as smooth as possible. Remember, too, that this is a long and emotionally charged road, so make sure your sell-side advisor is also someone you enjoy working with.

The best sell-side advisors bring more than technical expertise. They bring humanity and purpose to the process. While many in the field operate transactionally, focused solely on closing as many deals as fast as they can, a truly exceptional advisor approaches the role with a deeper purpose. They understand that it's not just about numbers or getting a "market multiple," but about guiding someone through a life-changing event with empathy, wisdom, and strategic insight.

An ideal advisor should have a background that goes beyond traditional investment banking. Look for someone who has been in the trenches—a former CEO *or business owner who understands what it's like to lead a business on a daily basis and lead businesses through a sale, and is someone who has both bought and sold companies, with a proven track record as an operator.*

This kind of hands-on experience provides a unique perspective. This sort of candidate has lived through the challenges of acquisitions from both sides of the table, which gives them a nuanced understanding of the process. They know how to steady the ship when the seller's emotions surge, and how to foster trust with buyers to create a collaborative environment. This balanced approach often results in smoother negotiations and, ultimately, a better strategic outcome for everyone involved.

At the same time, you need to pay special attention to the team backing up your advisor. Unfortunately, many firms perform a bait and switch. They lead with their top executives during the pitch, dazzling prospective clients with impressive presentations and well-crafted analytics. But once the deal is won, that star advisor steps aside and leaves the execution to a less-experienced team. Many of the biggest and most well-known investment banks in the world will take on middle-market deals, but their main focus is larger deals in the billions. So, the middle-market deals typically get junior teams, and their goal is to close as many transactions as possible to meet their numbers.

To avoid this, make sure the team you meet during the initial pitch will be the same team working with you through the entire process. A strong, cohesive team can make all the difference by ensuring continuity and focus from start to finish.

Finally, bear in mind that a reputable advisor should be able to provide direct client references—real business owners who can vouch for their expertise and integrity. If an entrepreneur is considering working with an advisory firm, they should ask for referrals and take the time to speak with past clients. One potential client I recently spoke with had been given a strong recommendation for another advisory firm but, after checking references, discovered multiple red flags that changed their decision. Due diligence up front is essential.

DON'T CUT COSTS

Many entrepreneurs are tempted to choose the firm with the lowest fees. However, this approach can backfire spectacularly. In M&A, as in life, you typically get what you pay for. Advisors with higher fee structures are often more motivated to bring their A-team to the table and deliver exceptional results. Those higher fees align their interests with yours and incentivize them to maximize the value of your deal. Conversely, choosing a lower-fee advisor can result in a less-experienced team and risk leaving significant money on the table.

When you're dealing with tens or hundreds of millions of dollars, quibbling over a small percentage difference in fees isn't just unwise; it's potentially disastrous. The premium you pay for top-tier expertise is an investment that often yields multiples in return—in terms of deal value, securing favorable terms, and getting the deal closed.

This holds true for businesses of many sizes. Whether your business generates $10 million in revenue or operates in the middle market of $50 million or more, the right advisor can make all the difference. For smaller businesses (those with less than $10 million in annual revenue), the process often falls to business brokers rather than full-fledged sell-side advisors. Brokers tend to take a transactional approach: listing the business for a set price, compiling basic information, and negotiating the deal. While this approach may suffice for smaller deals, it lacks the strategic depth and competitive edge of a true advisory process.

In contrast, businesses generating between $50 million and $1 billion or more will benefit greatly from a sell-side advisor. At this level, leaving even a few percentage points of value on the table could equate to millions of dollars lost. A skilled advisor can more than justify their fees by orchestrating comprehensive processes, competitive auctions, and well-executed outreach to find the best strategic home for the business, ensuring the full potential of the deal is realized.

FIND YOUR ADVISOR'S *WHY*

Understanding an advisor's deeper motivations can reveal whether they bring more than technical expertise to the table. The best advisors have a clear purpose—their own *why*—that transcends the transaction itself. My *why*, for example, is to help owners of privately held businesses achieve *their* why—and, of course, maximum valuation—moving them from Success to Significance™. To put it even more plainly, helping sellers achieve their personal desired outcomes and close 30 to 200, or even 300, percent higher than they were expecting is what lights me up and gets me out of bed in the morning.

The additional value an advisor can deliver often has a cascading effect. The incremental wealth unlocked in a well-executed deal frequently funds greater philanthropic efforts, supports communities, and/or strengthens family legacies. This sense of creating lasting, positive change energizes advisors who see their work as a way to multiply their contributions to the world.

When an advisor has a strong *why*, it's easier for them to stay the course, even when the process is long and complicated. Deals don't always follow a tidy timeline. I remember one transaction that took a whopping twenty-three months to close. It was a roller coaster, with alignment issues among shareholders and complications within the business itself. But my team never eased up, not on day one, and not on day seven hundred. Because we were all firmly rooted in our *why*s, in the end, we managed to align everyone's interests with the buyer's and create an incredibly successful outcome for all parties involved.

ASK THE TOUGH QUESTIONS

Entrepreneurs should feel empowered to ask tough, thoughtful questions when evaluating potential advisors. Asking about their purpose, their motivations, and the composition of their team isn't intrusive—it's smart. Questions like "Why are you in this business?" and "What drives your team?" and "Who exactly will be working on my deal?" can provide valuable insight into whether the advisor aligns with your goals and values.

When entrepreneurs consider selling their business, the first thing that many M&A advisors say is, "Send me your financials. What's your EBITDA?" They take a straightforward, transactional, numbers-first approach that feels impersonal and, frankly, a little mechanical. But the best advisors take a completely different route.

Why does the seller want to sell their business? What's their purpose? What are they trying to achieve? What are their *must-haves* and their *nice-to-haves*? Since you're reading this book, you may already know the answers—and that's incredibly powerful, because as we explained earlier, those insights frame the entire process and ensure that the deal aligns with the seller's goals, values, and vision for the future.

This level of personalization is what sets great advisors apart from the rest of the field. They're not checking off generic boxes or rushing to close a deal. Rather, they are crafting a process that reflects the seller's values and achieves outcomes that go beyond the dollar amount. For sellers, this means not only securing the best possible deal but also finding peace of mind knowing their business and its legacy are in good hands.

KNOW WHAT TO LOOK FOR *AND* WHAT TO AVOID

When choosing a sell-side advisor, spotting red flags can save you from all sorts of trouble. Let's look at a few that you need to be aware of.

First, while it's tempting to look for specialists in your industry (those who have done numerous deals in the same space), it's worth scrutinizing that choice. I know: The logic behind hiring a specialist seems sound. After all, they know the buyers, the companies, and the industry, inside and out. And, they've likely built an enormous list of contacts and can quickly pick up the phone to market your business. On the surface, it seems like a safer, faster option.

But here's where it gets tricky. If an advisor is *too* connected within the industry, particularly if they work for a multiservice firm that does buy-side deals, sell-side deals, consulting, capital raises, and more, they may not push as hard as they should for maximum value. These firms often have ongoing relationships with buyers, particularly private equity firms, which can create subtle conflicts of interest. The advisor might be motivated to keep the buyer happy because that buyer represents repeat business. In such cases, sellers may get an "industry market deal" rather than true strategic value, which means they're leaving dollars on the table.

Another concern with specialists is their tunnel vision. They may focus solely on buyers within the industry and overlook those in adjacent spaces or international markets. Casting a broader net, especially internationally, requires not only connections, but also a robust global network. Beware of firms that claim an international presence but rely on third-party partnerships rather than their own offices and employees. An advisor with genuine international reach and creativity in targeting buyers will generate better results. For example, a firm that has been around for decades has likely built a large database of buyers and knows how to reach the right decision-makers. That's important, because when it comes to selling a business, you want an advisor who excels at creating strategic value, not just someone who knows how to get market-level deals done.

In a similar vein, an advisor who focuses primarily or solely on private equity poses another potential red flag. While they offer legitimate opportunities, deals with private equity tend to close faster, which makes them attractive to advisors eager to close more deals in less time. If your advisor's buyer list skews heavily toward private equity, it's worth questioning whether they're prioritizing speed and ease over finding the best strategic fit.

At the same time, it's important to understand that investment bankers who are aligned with PE firms as buyers will work to get a good market deal done for the seller so that they may then also lead the future exit for the PE firm. That can lead to a big conflict. Yes, they will get a good "market" deal for the seller, but they won't get the maximum strategic valuation because that is against the need of the PE buyer to maximize their return with the future exit (which the investment banker hopes the PE firm will give them to lead). This occurs frequently and is how the market has evolved.

Transparency is another area where red flags can pop up. Many advisors and investment banks trumpet their deals, showcasing which companies they've sold to whom, often with elaborate tombstone plaques or announcements. While this is great for their marketing, it's not always in the best interest of their clients. Some sellers and even some buyers prefer confidentiality, whether for competitive reasons or personal privacy. Advisors who prioritize their own promotion over client discretion might not have their clients' best interests at heart.

Also, pay close attention to how you were approached by the advisor in the first place. If the initial contact came from a cold call or email claiming, "We have a buyer interested in your business," that's a major red flag. This dialing-for-deals approach often signals an operation focused on volume rather than quality. Such firms may be driven more by the needs of their existing buyers than by the interests of potential sellers. On top of that, if the person reaching out to you is a junior analyst or someone relatively inexperienced, it's a strong indicator that your deal will also be handled by a less-experienced team.

Remember, choosing the right sell-side advisor is about finding a partner who brings strategic thinking, creativity, and alignment with your goals. Avoid those who prioritize speed, volume, or their own marketing over your success. The difference between a mediocre deal and a great one often comes down to the advisor's approach and willingness to advocate fiercely for your best interests. Keep your eyes open for these red flags and trust your instincts—they're often your best guide in spotting the right fit.

AVOID SELLER SELF-SABOTAGE

Confidentiality is a top priority in every transaction. If word leaks that a company is for sale, it can destabilize employees, customers, and suppliers, causing unintended disruption. A good advisor will emphasize this from the outset—if a buyer breaches confidentiality, *they're out of the process*. Most buyers take this as seriously as sellers do. Private equity firms, corporate strategics, and public companies all rely on maintaining reputations of discretion. If a buyer becomes known for leaking deals, future sellers will refuse to work with them.

Even with confidentiality maintained, surprises are common when deals close—not just that a sale is happening, but *who the buyer is*. Many assume a direct competitor will be the acquirer, but often, the best buyer is outside the industry or in an adjacent market segment, offering complementary capabilities rather than direct overlap. These unexpected fits often lead to the best strategic outcomes and outlier value for the seller. Ignoring these types of buyers (or working with an advisor who ignores them) can prove costly.

That's not the only costly mistake sellers make. Remember, emotions run high during these transactions. Many entrepreneurs have devoted decades to building their companies, and when negotiations turn to valuations, leadership transitions, or post-sale roles, ego and pride can become obstacles. I've personally seen sellers get deeply offended over board seat offers or compensation packages, misinterpreting standard governance structures as personal slights.

One seller we worked with, after receiving a substantial offer for his company, expected to remain on as a board advisor. The buyer agreed but offered the same stipend they provide all their advisors—a nominal quarterly fee. The seller took this as an insult. "I'm worth more than $60,000 a year," he argued, failing to recognize that this wasn't about his personal value but the acquirer's existing structure. (Not only that, he was also going to be paid a nine-figure sum for his company.) Despite attempts to reframe the discussion, he ended up declining the board role altogether...and almost walked away from the sale as well.

Misunderstandings about valuation structures are also common. One seller we worked with assumed that on top of the sale price, the buyer would also pay (separately) for inventory, not realizing that market multiples already include inventory as part of needed working capital to run the business. When he learned this wasn't the case, he was ready to walk away, convinced he was being taken advantage of. It took both myself and his M&A attorney to explain that his expectations were incorrect—not because the buyer was shortchanging him, but because that's how business sales fundamentally work.

Moments like these illustrate why an advisor's role is not just financial, but psychological. To perform this role well, the advisor needs to be solely focused on the seller's needs. However, as I briefly mentioned in the introduction, one of the biggest mistakes sellers make is working with conflicted advisors—firms that represent both buyers and sellers in different deals. Many investment banks and M&A firms offer a full-service approach, handling buy-side and sell-side transactions while providing financing, accounting, due diligence, and consulting services to the buyer. While this may seem like a benefit, it creates an unavoidable conflict of interest.

DON'T SETTLE FOR "GOOD ENOUGH"

Imagine a real estate agent who represents both the seller and the buyer in a transaction. If that agent is good friends with the buyer, will they truly push for the highest possible price on behalf of the seller? Or will they focus on simply getting the deal done "at market," making sure the buyer is happy while offering just enough to satisfy the seller? The same conflict exists in the world of mergers and acquisitions.

A true sell-side advisor has one goal: *getting the best possible deal for the seller.* That means identifying and achieving strategic value, finding the best buyer(s), and ensuring all terms—not just price—are favorable. It means guiding the seller through the emotional aspects of the sale, helping them understand what's reasonable, and ensuring they don't let pride, misinterpretations, or unrealistic expectations sabotage a great outcome. This also helps the buyer get the strategic fit they're looking for, while at the same time providing a smoother process for all parties involved.

Remember, selling a business is rarely just a financial transaction—it's an emotional, strategic, and deeply personal process. Owners often have a long history with their companies, having built them from the ground up, and they want to ensure that the next chapter unfolds in the best possible way. Without the right guidance,

misunderstandings, misaligned expectations, and emo-
tional reactions can derail even the most promising
deals. That's where having a dedicated sell-side advisor
becomes so valuable.

Ultimately, selling your business is one of the most significant financial decisions you'll ever make. Why settle for
"good enough" when you could achieve something extraordinary? By broadening your perspective and partnering with
the right advisor, you set yourself up for a deal that not only
closes but delivers results that exceed your expectations.

HIROSHI

When he got back to his desk after lunch with Charles
and Alma, the first thing Hiroshi did was start research-
ing what made a good sell-side advisor. After sorting
through all the information he could find about investment bankers, sell-side advisors, and so on, he understood even more deeply why Charles kept talking about
having a "dedicated" sell-side advisor: To get the best
outcome, he needed someone who was focused solely
on representing *him*.

It was a little bit of sticker shock to see the fees
that advisors charged, but after talking to Charles and
Alma—one of whom had used an advisor, and one of

whom hadn't—he figured the right advisor would be more than worth it.

Excited, he started making a list of the questions he wanted to ask potential advisors when he met with them, including:

- "Why are you in this business?"
- "What drives your team?"
- "Who exactly will be working on my deal?"
- "What are your fees?" and...
- "What can I expect during the process?"

BUILDING A POWERHOUSE TEAM

JONATHAN

A S IMPORTANT AS THE RIGHT SELL-SIDE ADVI-
sor is, they aren't the only one you'll need in your corner
if you want a successful exit. Another key player—as I
learned firsthand—is a coach.

When I first stumbled into working with a coach, it
was a little surprising. Like many entrepreneurs, I believed I
could figure things out on my own, as long as I had enough grit
and determination. But an unexpected opportunity came my
way: a few free sessions with a coach. It sounded intriguing,
so I gave it a shot. Those sessions opened my eyes to something I hadn't fully appreciated before—the value of having
someone outside my bubble ask hard questions and provide
fresh perspectives.

I'll be honest: At first, I was skeptical that John, whose background was in banking, was the right coach for me. My business was in manufacturing, and I was knee-deep in the unique challenges that come with growing a company in that space. How could someone from banking possibly understand what I was dealing with? But I quickly realized that John didn't need to have lived my exact experience in order to be effective. In fact, his perspective, unburdened by the biases I carried, proved invaluable. He wasn't bogged down by the minutiae of manufacturing. Instead, he focused on strategy, decision-making, and helping me identify my own blind spots.

Did you know that, at the time of this writing, out of the thirty-two head coaches in the NFL, only nine are former players? When I first read that statistic, it floored me. But it makes sense. The best coaches don't necessarily need to have walked the same path as their players, just as coaches don't need to have operated in the exact same industry as their clients. Instead, they excel by offering clarity, asking powerful questions, and guiding their players to reach new heights. This was exactly what John brought to the table.

Another unexpected benefit of working with John was his connection to a broader network of coaches. He tapped into a collective brain trust of professionals with diverse expertise. If John encountered a challenge he hadn't faced before, he could consult with his network and bring back tailored advice. For me, this was a game-changer. I wasn't just hiring a coach; I was gaining access to an entire *ecosystem* of insights and support.

For any entrepreneur who is considering working with a coach—and I highly recommend you do, because they'll help you with both the day-to-day running of the company *and* the sale process—I encourage you to stay open-minded. Don't limit yourself to coaches who mirror your background. Some of the most valuable insights come from those who bring a fresh perspective, unclouded by the same biases and assumptions you carry.

Consider coaches who are part of network-based groups. These organizations bring not only individual expertise but also the collective wisdom of seasoned professionals who've tackled a wide range of challenges. It's like having an entire team working behind the scenes to help you succeed.

Finally, understand that coaching is a partnership. If something isn't working—whether it's the format, the cadence, or the approach—speak up. As I mentioned in the introduction, I did just that early on in my coaching relationship with John, and it made all the difference. A great coach will adapt and find ways to meet your needs while still pushing you to grow. Coaching isn't about following a rigid formula. It's about collaboration and finding what works for you. As John often said, "If a coach is in it for the money, it's not going to work. You have to love coaching and be driven by seeing others succeed." That passion was evident in every session, and it's one of the reasons his coaching practice thrived through referrals from satisfied clients like me.

STAY COACHABLE

For many entrepreneurs (myself included), the biggest challenge of working with a coach is *being coachable*. We're used to calling the shots and taking the lead. Letting someone else guide us can feel unnatural, even uncomfortable. But being coachable doesn't mean surrendering control. It means being open to new ideas, willing to listen, and committed to growth.

My time with John showed me that a great coach isn't there to tell you what to do. They are there to help you see the bigger picture, to challenge your assumptions, and to guide you toward making better decisions. Coaching taught me that the best answers often come from outside your own experience.

As an entrepreneur and business leader, you're expected to be the one with solutions. People come to you with problems, and you're the fixer. The decision-maker. So admitting that you don't have it all figured out can feel downright counterintuitive. But that humility, the willingness to admit you don't know everything, unlocks the real power of coaching.

A great coach isn't your boss. They don't bark orders. What they do is far more valuable. They guide you to uncover the answers already within you. More often than not, I found that I knew what I needed to do. Whether it was a tough conversation with an employee or deciding to let go of a problem client, the real issue wasn't knowledge but action. My coach provided a space where I could face those decisions head-on. He offered both accountability and reassurance that I was on the right path.

When I decided to sell my business, the role of my coach became even more significant. Selling a company is a very personal decision. After all, this is something you've poured years of your life into. Letting go, while exciting, can also be painful. John was there for me in those moments. He grounded me when the process felt overwhelming and helped me make decisions with clarity.

GET THE RIGHT TEAM FOR THE RIGHT STAGE

Even though I had gone through sale processes twice before, I knew if I wanted to achieve maximum valuation for Quicken Steel—and get all my other required outcomes—I needed the right people to guide me. My coach was an integral part of that equation.

John was focused on me—my mindset, my strategy, my well-being. Not only that, but he also helped me start thinking about the long-term implications of a sale well before we even began discussions with potential buyers. From preparing emotionally to addressing operational gaps that might affect valuation, our groundwork proved to be incredibly important.

I vividly remember the moment I received the first offer for my business. It was a number I never thought I'd see on paper, but John helped me navigate the initial euphoria and make sure I stayed focused on the big picture. Having him in my corner kept me grounded so I could make clearheaded decisions amid the whirlwind of activity.

The roles of a good coach and a sell-side advisor are beautifully complementary. A sell-side advisor is the tactical expert, the strategist who makes sure everything is aligned to achieve the best outcome. The best ones, like Andy and his team, also help their clients navigate the emotional part of the journey as much as possible. Your coach, on the other hand, is primarily focused on you. They're there to support your personal and strategic well-being, to help you manage the emotional weight of the process, and to ensure you're making decisions aligned with your long-term goals.

While the delineation of their roles wasn't strict, for the most part, my coach was my emotional anchor during the sale process, and my sell-side advisor was the architect of the deal. Selling a business is a highly specialized process, and while John helped me prepare for the personal and strategic challenges, the technical side required a whole different kind of expertise—expertise that Andy had.

Andy and his team handled everything from the beginning of the sale process right through to managing buyer outreach and negotiations. They understood my business inside and out, worked tirelessly to highlight its strengths, and presented it in a way that attracted serious offers. What impressed me most was how they thought beyond the obvious. Instead of limiting their focus to buyers in my industry, they reached out to adjacent sectors like home builders and modular home manufacturers. While I didn't end up selling to those buyers, their interest created a competitive environment that drove up the final sale price.

Fee structure was an area where Andy's transparency stood out. They used a tiered system, where they earned higher fees for exceeding expectations. When the deal closed, we ended up in the highest bracket, and I was happy to write that check. It was a big fee, but the value they brought to the table was so much bigger that it was absolutely worth it. And that's why I always say, don't skimp on a sell-side advisor! Their fees might seem steep, but a great advisor will more than pay for themselves by negotiating a better deal and making sure you avoid costly mistakes.

HIRE AN M&A SPECIALIST ATTORNEY

Another crucial member of your team is your attorney. A common mistake is relying on a general business attorney instead of hiring one who is an M&A specialist. The lawyer who helped you set up an LLC or drafted contracts isn't necessarily the right fit for representing you in a complex acquisition.

M&A transactions involve unique legal nuances, and having an attorney with direct experience in these deals can make a huge difference in how smoothly the process unfolds.

I had a trusted friend in YPO who had sold his company a few years before me. He recommended an attorney out of Jacksonville—a top-tier firm, highly qualified, and very expensive. You get what you pay for, and in a deal of this magnitude, hiring the right legal counsel is an investment worth making.

Finding the right attorney should be a team decision, so be sure to involve your sell-side advisor, your business coach, and other trusted mentors. If possible, it's best to bring in an M&A attorney early in the process. This ensures that when the time comes to sell, all legal considerations have already been addressed.

However, one lesson I learned the hard way is that it's not just about legal expertise—it's also about how your attorney represents you in negotiations. My attorneys were highly competent and did an excellent job of protecting my interests, but I was disappointed with how they treated the other parties involved. At one of the most stressful times in my life, I found myself watching my legal team interact in a way that didn't align with my values. They were aggressive to the point of alienating key people, including members of my sell-side advisor team.

Looking back, I would still prioritize expertise, but I would also pay closer attention to how they communicate and deal with people. When an attorney represents you, their behavior reflects on you. If they are dismissive, abrasive, or combative, it can create unnecessary tension and even risk derailing the deal.

This is why checking references *thoroughly* is so important. Don't just assume that because an attorney comes highly recommended, they are the right fit for you. Take the time to talk to previous clients, and ask those references not just about the prospective attorney's legal skills, but about how they handle negotiations and people.

Ultimately, laying the groundwork for a successful exit includes building the right team. Getting a great sell-side advisor, a great coach, and a great attorney in your corner will help make what can be an arduous process into something far easier—and far more profitable.

CHARLES

Charles was excited: He was meeting with Hiroshi one-on-one again to talk about some of the strategies he used to get his successful outcome. As he drove over to the restaurant where he was meeting his friend for dinner, he started thinking about the biggest piece of advice he could give Hiroshi. He knew that, like a lot of entrepreneurs, Hiroshi often thought that he could handle things on his own. Charles had felt like that a lot, too, so he understood. However, Charles also knew that, like a lot of entrepreneurs, Hiroshi hadn't sold a business before. Trying to go it alone meant running the very real risk of leaving money on the table.

He realized that while it wouldn't be his only piece of advice, the biggest point he wanted Hiroshi to understand was simply that he needed a good team to help him. After all, having been through a sale himself, Charles would never consider doing it on his own. With the right sell-side advisor, a supportive coach, and a great attorney, he knew that Hiroshi would find the exit process to be a manageable journey worth every step.

TELLING THE RIGHT STORY FOR BUYERS

JONATHAN

A T THIS POINT, YOU'VE DONE A LOT OF PREPA-
ration: You've gotten clear on your *why*, identified your
must-haves and *nice-to-haves*, and built a great team. But
you still have a long way to go before your sell-side advisor can start seeking out and engaging buyers.

One of the first things Andy and his team did to start building interest among prospective buyers was to prepare a teaser,
which is an anonymous, high-level overview of the business
designed to spark interest among prospective buyers. Once
that went out, interested parties could sign nondisclosure
agreements (NDAs), and we would then provide them with
the Confidential Information Memorandum (CIM). A CIM

is essentially a full presentation that details the compelling opportunity the business represents.

I had heard from numerous people that getting the CIM right was extremely important, and it needed to present the business in a way that was not only accurate but also compelling. It had to tell a story—a story of past success, current stability, and future potential.

Andy and his team played a critical role in gathering all the necessary information for the CIM. Through multiple calls and deep discussions, they were able to grasp the business at an impressive level. It was remarkable how well they understood not just the basics of what we did, but also the intricacies of our operations. They came in with a clear vision for how the CIM should be presented to tell our story to prospective buyers. While there wasn't necessarily a strict template, there was a structured approach that made sense. My job was to make sure all the key details about the business were included. Andy's team handled the layout and final presentation, but I had to provide the substance.

One of the biggest challenges in creating the CIM was identifying what made our business special. As a founder, it's easy to overlook the uniqueness of day-to-day operations because they feel routine. For example, our automated order processing system was something we had built over time, and to us, it was just how things worked. But Andy helped us recognize that this system was actually a huge differentiator.

Our enterprise resource planning (ERP) system allowed us to process orders with limited human interaction, automatically coordinating inventory, production, and logistics. Barcode scanning, automated sorting, and seamless integration between departments created an efficient operation. To us, it was standard. To a buyer, it demonstrated *scalability*—a critical factor in assessing a company's potential.

That's where Andy's expertise came in. He would drill down into details by asking the right questions, such as "How does it connect to other systems? Why did you build it this way?"

These questions were invaluable, because we wanted a buyer to know they weren't just purchasing a company; they were acquiring a well-oiled machine, one that was built to scale without being hindered by manual bottlenecks.

Another major component of the CIM was demonstrating the business's market reach. Andy and his team wanted to show both where we were and where we could go. We mapped out our sales footprint—not just local or regional sales, but national and even international distribution. Our dealer network extended across the US, and we had done business in locations as far away as Cuba, Hawaii, and Alaska. Visually representing that reach made it clear that we weren't just a small Georgia-based company—we had already expanded significantly, with even more room to grow.

The CIM also included financial summaries, past performance data, and future projections. Rather than simply plugging in historical growth rates, we developed a pro forma financial model that accounted for real-world factors, such as personnel expansion, equipment upgrades, additional equipment, geographic scaling, and industry trends like steel price fluctuations. We wanted to give buyers a high-level snapshot of where the business had been and where it could scale to with the right investment and leadership.

KEEP THE SALE UNDER WRAPS

One of the most difficult parts of putting the CIM together was gathering the needed information without alerting employees. It's standard practice to keep a business sale confidential until it's finalized. Announcing too early can create uncertainty and unrest among staff.

This presented a challenge. Potential buyers want to understand the company inside and out, but we couldn't exactly have a parade of visitors touring the facility. We needed a way to give buyers a full understanding of the business without raising suspicions internally.

That's when Andy and I came up with an idea based on his prior experience—*we would offer prospective buyers a virtual tour*. I had previously worked with a video production team to create marketing videos, so I brought them in again under the same premise. Employees were used to seeing cameras around, so it didn't raise any red flags.

I recorded a short (around three minutes) walk-through video where I personally guided viewers through the business. I started in the office, moved through manufacturing, showcased inventory storage, highlighted equipment and logistics, and demonstrated how orders were processed and fulfilled.

The video became an integral part of the CIM. We embedded it in the CIM itself so buyers could get a firsthand look at the business without setting foot on-site. The response was overwhelmingly positive. Several buyers said it gave them a much better feel for the company and made them more comfortable moving forward.

At its core, the CIM is a marketing document. It's the story of your business strategically framed to show its strengths, opportunities, and scalability. Creating it took longer than I expected, but when it was done, I understood why. It was a quality piece of work, carefully crafted to put our business in the best possible light.

At the end of the day, the CIM is your company's sales pitch, and just like any great pitch, it needs to be clear, compelling, and strategic. If done correctly, it can be the difference between attracting serious buyers and wasting time with tire-kickers.

HELP YOUR ADVISOR CREATE A COMPELLING CIM

Once the CIM was distributed, Andy and his team held deep conversations with potential buyers, both to filter out those who weren't serious and to learn why each buyer considered themselves to be a great home for my business. Buyers who remained engaged submitted indications of interest (IOIs), essentially pitching themselves to us and explaining why they would be the right fit. This process gave us a clear understanding of the market's perception of our business and helped us gauge the best path forward.

After learning and collaborating with Andy and his team, I have a few key tips for how you can help your advisor create the best possible CIM:

1. **Don't underestimate your unique processes.** What seems normal to you might be a game-changer for a buyer. What's your secret sauce? Your *Rembrandts in the Attic*?

2. **Show, don't just tell.** Use visuals, maps, and even video to make your business tangible.

3. **Think like a buyer.** What questions would you ask if you were acquiring this company? And what are your unique value drivers for each buyer? Address those proactively.

4. **Keep the sale confidential.** Find creative ways to give buyers the information they need without disrupting operations.

The CIM is often one of the most challenging parts of the entire sale process. In fact, I would put it in the top three, but to be fair, everything about selling a business felt difficult at times. It helps a lot if you have the right team. Andy's group, my coach, and outsourced experts made the process far more manageable for us. Without them, I would have felt completely isolated and overwhelmed. While no one inside my company knew about the sale at that point in the process, I had a strong team of advisors who had been through the process before and knew exactly what needed to happen.

The bottom line: Here, as with so many other parts of the process, I can say unequivocally that *going it alone is a mistake*. Trying to navigate a sale without expert guidance can be overwhelming. We outsourced financial reporting and projections, CIM development, and the entire marketing and outreach process. Andy's firm handled everything from drafting the teaser and CIM to vetting potential buyers. Even though I had prior experience with selling companies, if I had tried to manage all of that internally, it would have been impossible, especially while keeping the sale confidential. Because I was willing to get outside help, though, I ended up getting more than three times my initial projection.

Selling a business is ultimately a strategic process that requires strong positioning, compelling storytelling, and a well-assembled team. The CIM is one of the most challenging parts of the journey, but it is also one of the most valuable tools in securing the right buyer. It pays to get it right.

Because it's so important, I think it's worth digging into the CIM a bit more. The next chapter offers additional detail about it, this time from a sell-side advisor's perspective.

CHARLES AND HIROSHI

"Hey, Charles, can I ask you one more thing?" Hiroshi said as they were wrapping up their meal.

"Of course," he replied.

"I've read a lot about the CIM. Is that something I put together? Or will my advisor do it? Either way, what do you think are the most important points I should know to make sure it's as powerful as possible?"

"Those are great questions, Hiroshi," Charles said. "My dedicated sell-side advisor put the CIM together, but it was with my input. I think the most important thing you can do to help your advisor craft a great CIM is to think about what your company's competitive advantages are. I know you have systems in place that automate *everything*, which I imagine would be very attractive to prospective buyers. I also know that you've focused on recession-proofing the business by creating multiple revenue streams for things that people need no matter what the economy is doing. Those are the sort of things that your advisor might want to highlight in the CIM. I suggest taking some time to think about other key differentiators to your business, so you can help your advisor create a compelling story that will entice prospective buyers."

"That's super helpful, Charles—thanks!" Hiroshi said. "I'm so close to the business, though, that it's kind of hard to figure out what the key differentiators are."

"I get it," he replied. "So try this: Think like your buyer. What sort of concerns might they have, and what solutions have you created to address those concerns? That might help you get started. And don't be afraid to talk to your advisor about this stuff. They'll bring a fresh perspective to your business and help you identify the things that will really make prospective buyers sit up and take notice."

Hiroshi knew that his advisor would ask him insightful questions to draw the necessary information out of him, but he was so excited that he didn't want to wait. As soon as he got back to his desk, he grabbed his trusty pad and pen and started writing.

MAKE YOUR CODE NAME YOUR ANCHOR

When selling a business, confidentiality is everything. At this stage, every document, including teasers, CIMs, and financials, must be handled with discretion. To keep things under wraps, Andy and his team assign a code name to the sale, a common practice in mergers and acquisitions. It can be anything—Project Blue Sky, Project Green Tree—something neutral that wouldn't give the company away or allow prospective buyers to guess who the company is.

I remember Andy asking me early on, "Jonathan, we need to name this project. What do you want to call it?" Without hesitation, I answered, "Project Ebenezer."

Andy didn't question it. He just said, "Sounds good," and from that moment forward, every email, document, and phone call referenced Project Ebenezer. It probably didn't mean much to anyone else, but for me, it carried a deep significance.

The name comes from a story in the Old Testament (1 Samuel 7), when the Israelites were under constant threat from the Philistines. For years, they had drifted away from God, but in a moment of surrender, they turned back to Him. The prophet Samuel led them in repentance, and as they gathered to seek God's help, the Philistine army advanced, ready to crush them.

At that moment, Samuel sacrificed a lamb and cried out to God for deliverance. In response, a great thunder erupted from the heavens, throwing the Philistine army into complete confusion. The Israelites seized the opportunity, won a decisive victory, and reclaimed their strength.

To commemorate the moment, Samuel set up a stone and named it Ebenezer, which means "Up until now, God has helped us." It was a marker of trust, provision, and divine help—a reminder that they had not walked alone.

That was exactly how I felt in the early stages of selling my business. I had done everything I could to build something valuable, but now I was stepping into unknown territory, a process filled with uncertainty and high stakes. I needed an anchor—an acknowledgment that I was not walking alone. The name Ebenezer became just that.

Every time I saw an email or document labeled Project Ebenezer, it reminded me: *Up until now, God has helped us. And He's not done yet.*

This didn't change the fact that selling the business was incredibly difficult. It was still a roller coaster of negotiations, financial reviews, and high-pressure decisions. But having that name, that simple yet powerful reminder, helped keep me grounded. It reminded me that I wasn't doing this alone, and that I didn't have to carry the weight of the process entirely on my own shoulders.

I believe that in any major life transition, whether it's selling a business, starting something new, or navigating uncertainty, it's important to have anchors, things that remind you why you started and give you the confidence to keep moving forward. For me, that anchor was my faith. For someone else, it might be a mentor, a guiding principle, or a core belief. Whatever it is, hold onto it. Because when the process gets overwhelming—and it will—you need something to fall back on.

Looking back, the sale was an exercise in character-building. It tested me in ways I never expected, but it also strengthened my ability to trust the process, to let go of what I couldn't control, and to move forward with confidence. And every time I heard Project Ebenezer, it was a reminder: *Up until now, we've been helped. And we will be carried through the rest.*

CAPTURE THE ESSENCE OF THE BUSINESS

ANDY

SELLING A COMPANY IS A LOT LIKE TELLING A good story. It's not just about financials or spreadsheets but capturing the essence of where the company has been, how it got to its current success, and, most importantly, what its future could look like in the right hands. A great sell-side advisor helps craft and share this story in a way that excites potential suitors and creates competitive tension, driving up value for the seller (and also delivering win–win strategic value for the buyer).

To do this, you need the right tools. One of the most important of these tools is the CIM. You can think of the CIM as the business's résumé—only instead of being crammed with every tiny detail, it should tell a clear and concise story. Some advisory firms overload their CIMs with data: sixty, seventy, even one hundred pages of charts, numbers, and minutiae. I don't like that approach; it's overwhelming and misses the point. A great CIM distills the narrative into twenty to thirty pages. It prioritizes visual appeal, clarity, easy-to-understand bullet points, and strategic detail. Those elements ensure that the key strengths of the business stand out—covering the company's history, sales, customers, suppliers, operations, people, and financials, plus a compelling story about *why* the business is such a great opportunity, leaving deeper dives for due diligence. When done well, it sparks excitement and curiosity without drowning the buyer in unnecessary detail.

The CIM is the primary document used to present the business in an appealing way to serious buyers. It provides enough information for a potential buyer to craft a well-informed preliminary offer—often before conducting site visits or deep due diligence. The best CIMs balance detail with readability, avoiding an overwhelming data dump that could deter potential buyers.

As a prior CEO and strategic buyer who received and read hundreds of CIMs, I developed the viewpoint that the most effective CIM is one that lets a potential buyer scan it in five minutes and walk away thinking, *This is a great business that we need to buy. I'm going to have the team dig into deeper due diligence to confirm the opportunity and make it happen.*

CREATE A STRONG CIM

Your sell-side advisor will handle creating the CIM, but it's important to understand the specifics of what makes a CIM strong so you can help them craft a compelling document.

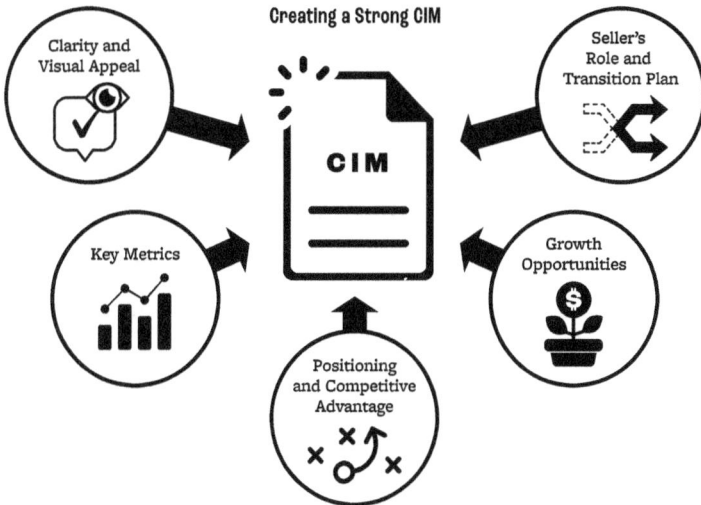

Creating a Strong CIM

1. CLARITY AND VISUAL APPEAL

A strong CIM is structured, engaging, and easy to navigate. Key business attributes should jump off the page, immediately signaling why the company is a valuable opportunity.

2. KEY FINANCIAL AND BUSINESS METRICS

The CIM includes detailed financial summaries, revenue/profit trends, and projections, but does not overwhelm buyers with unnecessary minutiae. The financial data should support the company's growth narrative and justify its valuation.

3. INDUSTRY POSITIONING AND COMPETITIVE ADVANTAGE

The document highlights the market position, valuable customer base, and differentiators that make the business attractive. It outlines why the business has growth potential, strategic barriers to entry (moats), and strategic value for a buyer.

4. GROWTH OPPORTUNITIES

Buyers need to see what's next for the company. The CIM presents scalability, expansion potential, potential acquisitions, and operational efficiencies that could be leveraged post-acquisition.

5. SELLER'S ROLE AND TRANSITION PLAN

If the owner is stepping away post-sale, buyers want to know who will lead the company going forward. This section should highlight a strong management team and/or organizational structure, or outline a transition plan to reassure buyers of continuity.

A well-structured CIM should encourage buyers to fall in love with the business while providing sufficient data to validate its value. It builds on the teaser, offering deeper insights into the company's financials, operations, and strategic positioning, but without overwhelming buyers with excessive details up front. Additional information is provided during follow-up meetings, due diligence, the virtual data room, and Q&A sessions.

Ultimately, the CIM is a storytelling tool, carefully crafted to position the business as an attractive, high-value investment. When done correctly, it becomes the foundation for negotiations, offers, and ultimately, a successful sale.

MASTER THE ELEMENTS OF THE CIM

Every CIM is tailored to the unique attributes of the business being sold. While there is no rigid template, most CIMs include the following sections.

COMPANY OVERVIEW

A clear and compelling summary of what the company does and how it operates. This section provides buyers with an understanding of the business model and industry positioning. It should also answer key questions, including:

- What does the business do?
- How does it do it?
- Why is the business uniquely successful?
- Why is the future sustainable and bright?
- Why is this a compelling strategic acquisition?

FINANCIALS

Detailed financial summaries, typically placed at the back of the document. This includes balance sheets, profit and loss statements, forecasts, and adjustments from the quality of earnings (QofE) report. If adjustments were made (e.g., normalizing earnings by removing nonrecurring expenses), they should be clearly outlined.

OPERATIONS AND COMPETITIVE ADVANTAGE

The secret sauce of the business—what sets it apart. This could be proprietary technology, its sales channel(s), customers, geographic location(s), unique processes, strong supplier relationships, or an innovative approach to market.

TECHNOLOGY AND SYSTEMS

If the company has significant technology investments, CRM systems, or ERP systems, or uses AI and/or business intelligence to support scalability, these are highlighted.

COMPETITIVE LANDSCAPE

A detailed look at competitors and where the company stands in comparison. Interestingly, some of these competitors may also be potential buyers, meaning that including them in the CIM creates competitive tension.

SALES AND COST STRUCTURE

Buyers will want to see sales and margin by product, customer, channel, and segment to understand revenue and profit drivers. They'll also want to see whether sales are subscription, recurring, or project-based. Likewise, they'll need a breakdown of cost structure, including material costs and supplier relationships. In Jonathan's case, steel was a major cost driver, so his company's CIM needed to show how price fluctuations were handled—for example, whether increases were passed on to customers or cost savings were retained as additional margin.

FACILITIES AND GROWTH POTENTIAL

Information on manufacturing or office locations, equipment, and potential for scaling operations. For Jonathan, the ability to expand from a regional player to a national manufacturer was a key selling point, so we made sure to emphasize it in his CIM. His buyer had the infrastructure in place to support that expansion, making the acquisition even more valuable.

TEAM AND CULTURE

A well-structured management team is a huge value driver. If a company has long-tenured employees, low turnover, and a strong culture, those aspects should be highlighted. Buyers want stability and confidence that key personnel will stay on after the sale.

FORECAST AND GROWTH PROJECTIONS

Buyers need to understand where the business is headed. Are revenue and profit forecasts backed by a strong backlog? Or are they speculative? The CIM must support projections (both backlog and pipeline) with data to show whether growth is already in motion or dependent on uncertain factors.

FOLLOW A STRATEGIC SEQUENCE

The CIM is not sent to every interested party. A well-run process follows a strategic sequence:

1. **Teaser Distribution:** Sent on a no-name basis to protect confidentiality to a preapproved, targeted list of potential buyers. Some M&A advisory firms cast a wide net (especially to private equity), but a more focused approach prioritizes buyers with real strategic alignment.

2. **NDA Signing:** Only after a buyer signs an NDA do they gain access to the CIM.

3. **Selective Disclosure:** If a potential buyer is a direct competitor, some details may be redacted—such as customer names, pricing details, or sensitive proprietary information. Buyers may receive modified

versions of the CIM, with uniquely crafted compelling stories, until they demonstrate strong interest and move further in the process.

HELP ENSURE YOUR CIM IS EFFECTIVE

While sell-side advisors lead the CIM development, sellers play a crucial role in ensuring it accurately reflects the business's strengths. Here's how to help ensure the CIM is as powerful and compelling to buyers as possible.

CLARIFY KEY DIFFERENTIATORS

The advisor can frame the business well, but no one understands the company's strengths better than the founder (or its current leader). Sellers should work closely with advisors to ensure the company's competitive advantages are clearly articulated. A good advisor will help with this by asking the *right* questions to develop a strong and engaging summary and story for the business.

ENSURE DATA READINESS

Buyers expect clean, organized financials. Entrepreneurs should be proactive in tracking financial data, revenue streams, costs, and operational efficiencies, making it easier for advisors to present the business in the best possible light.

THINK LIKE A BUYER

Sellers should anticipate buyer concerns. If the business has risks—such as customer concentration, dependency on key suppliers, or a lack of leadership depth—these should be acknowledged and addressed up front.

BE TRANSPARENT ABOUT FINANCIAL ADJUSTMENTS

Many business owners run personal expenses through the company. Buyers expect this, but sellers need to consistently track and categorize these expenses so they can be easily adjusted in the QofE report. This ensures transparency and credibility during due diligence.

SUPPORT THE STRATEGIC NARRATIVE

If growth potential is a major selling point, sellers should work with their advisor to substantiate projections. If expansion is possible, what will it take? If sales are growing, is that momentum sustainable? A CIM that presents a realistic, well-supported growth story will command stronger offers.

A well-crafted CIM is a strategic sales document that presents the business in the best possible light while maintaining credibility. It shouldn't be a "data dump." The right balance of detail and clarity ensures that buyers quickly grasp the company's value and become excited about its potential.

By working closely with an advisor, entrepreneurs can help shape a CIM that attracts serious buyers, drives competition, and ultimately leads to a successful deal.

GO FROM CIM TO INITIAL OFFERS

From the time the CIM is distributed, the process of receiving initial offers typically takes four to eight weeks. The sale process is typically structured in two primary stages:

1. **Submission of Initial Offers**: Buyers present their opening offers based on the information provided in the CIM, follow-up discussions, and initial due diligence. These offers outline initial valuation, deal structure, and key terms, such as whether the deal consists of 100 percent cash, a combination of cash and seller equity rollover, seller financing, or an earnout structure. The initial offers also indicate what additional due diligence will be required and the buyer's ability to fund the acquisition. Finally, they provide insight as to why the buyer is the *best* home for the business.

2. **Selection and Negotiation**: The seller and their advisors review the initial offers, evaluating both financial terms and strategic fit. A strong offer isn't

just about the highest price—it's also about finding the right buyer. Factors such as cultural alignment, growth potential, and the buyer's long-term plans for the business play a crucial role.

If one buyer stands out as the ideal choice but their valuation is not the highest, the negotiation strategy shifts. Rather than simply accepting the best initial offer, a good sell-side advisor engages the buyers in discussions to better understand their lower valuation, then provide them support to make their offer more competitive. Buyers must articulate what makes them uniquely positioned to take the business to the next level— whether it's through supply chain integration, access to a new customer base, cross-selling, or complementary technology.

Once this strategic value is identified, negotiations intensify. Buyers are encouraged to adjust their offers to reflect the true worth of the business, considering not just market multiples but also the unique transformative synergies the acquisition will create. This competitive dynamic is often referred to as a soft auction, where multiple interested parties drive the final price upward to achieve the strategic advantages they need.

INCREASE VALUATION WITH THE RIGHT PROCESS

Jonathan's sale process is a clear example of how strategic negotiations—of which the CIM is a key piece—maximize value. The buyer's initial offer came in at a very respectable amount (one that far exceeded our initial estimate of what the business was worth based on typical market multiples), but through targeted discussions and competitive tension, the final sale price was another 33 *percent higher* than that—and more than 50 percent higher than what many of the initial "market" offers from other prospective buyers had been.

This was not an anomaly. In nearly every structured M&A process our clients go through, the winning bid far exceeds the initial round of offers. Buyers start at market value or slightly above, but as the process unfolds and they realize the full potential of the business, they are willing to significantly increase their bids to secure a deal that creates strategic value for them.

This approach ensures that businesses are not just sold at typical industry market values (like many sell-side advisors do) but at their true worth to the right buyer. By fostering competition, highlighting strategic synergies, and leveraging the power of negotiation, sellers can achieve substantially higher valuations than they might have initially expected.

HIROSHI

Setting his pen down, Hiroshi stared at what he had written. After talking to Charles, he had written a lot about the systems he had put in place to automate everything in his business and the revenue streams he had created to position the business to thrive in any economy.

It was a good start, but Hiroshi wondered what else he should talk about. Picking up the phone, he called Charles and shared what he had written so far.

"That's a great start, Hiroshi! I know when you hire an advisor, they'll be able to ask you exactly the right questions to draw out specific things that set your business apart, but I do remember that my advisor and I discussed my competitive landscape, my sales and cost structure, my facilities and their growth potential, my management team and company culture, and my growth projections. You can jot some things down about all of that, and together, you and the advisor you hire can build a compelling story about where your business was, where it is now, and where it's going."

"Makes sense," Hiroshi said. "I'll get started right now!"

SEVEN

SORTING THROUGH YOUR OPTIONS

JONATHAN

ONCE THE CIM GOES OUT, THINGS GET MORE serious. When the meetings with interested buyers start, excitement starts spiking—but so do your nerves. It's a lot to handle. I've been through it multiple times, and I can tell you that preparation, mindset, and guidance are key. When those initial meetings start occurring, you need to be ready to mentally and emotionally engage in a process that will test you on every level.

We had ten serious buyers at the indication of interest (IOI) stage. During these calls and virtual/video meetings, most of which were conducted via Zoom, the buyers wanted to understand the business, meet me, and ask a lot of questions. These weren't casual chats. They were fact-finding missions for the buyers and performance moments for me.

From the seller's perspective, these meetings are sales pitches, but not in the traditional sense. As Andy explained to me, you're not just selling your business. You're selling yourself as a credible and competent owner who has built something of real value. Buyers will pick up on your energy and engagement. They'll also look for *founder risk* (which, if you'll recall, essentially means you *are* the business). If you're emotionally detached, you seem unsure about your own business, or the company relies too heavily on you to operate, they'll sense it immediately. Confidence, clarity, and preparation are everything.

PREPARE FOR BUYER INTERACTIONS

Once the call starts, you're essentially in "performance mode," so before each call, I made sure to rehearse. However, it's not about being overly polished or coming across as salesy. Buyers appreciate genuine answers and honesty. If I didn't know the answer to a question, I didn't guess or bluff. Instead, I noted it and promised to follow up with accurate information. That honesty builds trust.

Andy and his team were instrumental in this phase. They'd already had their own conversations with the buyers and knew what hot-button issues might come up. They prepared me by sharing the buyers' main concerns and interests, which gave me a huge advantage. For example, one buyer was particularly focused on our employee retention rates. Knowing that in advance, I prepared specific data and anecdotal examples to highlight the culture we'd built. That kind of preparation not only answered their questions but also demonstrated that I was deeply engaged with the business.

With ten buyers in the mix, there were a lot of conversations. We spaced them out—just two or three calls in a day—but by the time you're on your tenth call, it can start to feel repetitive. For the buyer, it's their first impression of you and your business, but for you, it might feel like you're stuck on repeat. Staying fresh and energized for each conversation is critically important.

To keep my energy up, I followed the advice of my coach and Andy. First, I reminded myself of the stakes. Every conversation mattered. Each buyer was a potential path to a successful sale, and that perspective helped me stay motivated. Second, I tried to find a moment of quiet before each call to reset mentally. A quick walk or even just a few minutes of stillness made a big difference.

Andy also recommended that I work with a presentation/communications consultant, an expert who later helped me refine my skills for the in-person management presentations. Even before that, though, I still treated the initial buyer calls with seriousness. Remember, your demeanor and preparation in these early interactions set the tone for everything that follows.

My advice for navigating this part of the process successfully: Be yourself, but be the best-prepared version of yourself possible. Buyers are evaluating not just the business but also the person behind it. They're looking for someone who believes in what they've built, who knows the details, and who is willing to engage openly and honestly.

Yes, it's draining. Yes, it's repetitive. But it's also an opportunity to showcase everything you've worked so hard to create. If you approach it with the right mindset, it can be one of the most rewarding parts of the entrepreneurial journey.

Bear in mind, too, that these calls are just the beginning. The deeper dive, which includes management presentations, site visits, and final negotiations, comes later. For now, you are setting the stage for what's to come.

STAY RESILIENT AND ENGAGED

After those initial calls, Andy and his team distilled the feedback and presented the IOIs to me. This is where things can get emotionally charged. The IOIs were more than price tags. They included terms like owner financing, equity rollover, earnouts, and/or contingent payments based on future performance. It was a lot to process, and I quickly realized why it was so important to have clear *must-haves* and *nice-to-haves* established from the start.

For me, one nonnegotiable was that I wasn't going to stay and run the business on-site. I'd consider an off-site role for a limited period of time, but I wasn't going to commit to being there day-to-day. That clarity saved me from second-guessing myself when offers started rolling in, even when some were tempting enough to make me reconsider.

But not all offers are created equal. Some of the early offers were, frankly, insulting—low-ball figures that didn't come close to the value I knew we had built. Those were gut punches. When you're putting your heart and soul into this process and someone undervalues your work, it stings. Andy and my coach kept reminding me to keep my focus on the bigger picture and not let a few bad offers derail my confidence.

One of the hardest parts of this stage was managing my expectations. Over the months leading up to the offers, the business had grown significantly. Revenue and profits were climbing, and as a result, my valuation expectations started to creep higher. But I tempered those expectations with a clear-eyed view of reality: While it's good to have faith in what your business is worth, it's also important to stay grounded. Greed can cloud your judgment if you're not careful.

At the start of the process, I had made a conservative estimate of what the business might sell for. When I started working with Andy, though, we increased that number by more than 50 percent for a strategic valuation versus a typical industry/market valuation. Based on his vast experience and real-time market knowledge, Andy thought the business was realistically worth the higher valuation to a strategic buyer. After discussing it with him, I agreed.

Then, months later, due to greatly increased sales and profits, we saw the potential for something even greater. I wrote down a stretch goal that was 50 percent higher than the already increased figure. It was a number that, on the surface, felt like a leap of faith. However, Andy and I believed it was achievable—we just needed to grow significantly between that point and when we closed, all while attracting the right strategic buyers. We knew it would be hard, but doable.

When the IOIs came in, we had several offers in the mid range. Andy went to work running a competitive auction and negotiating with the buyers. The negotiations were successful and, eventually, two of the prospective buyers reached valuations that were 33 percent higher than my stretch goal, and more than 200 *percent higher* than my initial estimate. It was exhilarating, but also daunting. These were nonbinding offers—just initial indications of interest, which meant there was still a long way to go. It wasn't a done deal until the money hit the account, and I knew plenty could still go wrong.

My daughter Faith played a significant role in keeping me centered. I had written down that stretch goal with intention and backed it with the Bible verse that was becoming a mantra: *A good man leaves an inheritance to his children's children.* For me, that number represented security for my daughter and peace of mind for my family. It anchored me during moments of doubt and reminded me why I was pushing forward.

After reviewing the IOIs, Andy and I narrowed down the list to four finalists. That set the stage for the next phase: the management presentations. These were in-person meetings where I presented the business in detail, tailored to each buyer's interests. We scheduled two presentations per day over two days, each one lasting three to four hours, preceded or followed by meals with the buyers.

Those days were incredibly exhausting, but they were also the culmination of everything we'd worked toward. Standing in front of those buyers, I knew the preparation, resilience, and faith that had carried me through the earlier stages were paying off.

MANAGE THE TRANSITION

One of the trickiest parts of selling your business, particularly at this stage, is managing the transition for your team without tipping them off too early. When I decided to sell my company, I faced a delicate balance between keeping the business running smoothly and preparing my leadership team for what was coming. Sharing the news too soon wasn't an option, but neither was letting them remain unprepared for the eventual change.

About six months before the sale closed, I enlisted my coach, John, to start working with two key leaders in my business. While they had no idea the business was being sold, John did, and that knowledge allowed him to guide them in ways that subtly prepared them for the future. He became a voice of reason and support, helping them navigate day-to-day challenges and grow into stronger leaders. This was incredibly important because my focus started to split between running the business and managing the sale process.

When the time came to finally tell my team about the sale, having John there was invaluable. He brought an experienced and trusted perspective to the conversation, reassuring them that this was a natural part of a business's evolution. His involvement gave them confidence—not just in me, but in their own ability to handle the changes ahead.

He continued to work with them even after the sale, offering guidance as they adapted to new ownership and making sure the transition went as smoothly as possible. That continuity not only benefited my team, but it also became a major selling point for the buyers, who saw the value in having a coach who already understood the business and its people.

And of course, throughout the process, John helped me stay focused on what mattered most: keeping the business running and maintaining its growth trajectory.

SORTING THROUGH YOUR OPTIONS

LEAVE ROOM FOR FAITH

Throughout my entrepreneurial journey, especially during the sale of Quicken Steel, I learned the necessary balance between effort and faith. As entrepreneurs, we hear a lot about "hustle culture." This means business owners working long hours, pushing harder, and grinding through the stress. While hard work is essential, of course, it's not the whole story. Success isn't just about relentless effort. It's also about working with purpose and leaving room for faith and trust.

There's a Bible passage I often think about:

> *"Whatever your hand finds to do, do it with all your might"*
> *(Ecclesiastes 9:10).*

To me, that verse isn't telling us to embrace stress or anxiety, but to give our best effort with clarity and focus. That was the foundation of my approach to selling my business. I did everything I could to prepare, from hiring the right advisors to driving growth, but I also reminded myself to step back, breathe, and trust the process.

When the process became overwhelming, I leaned on daily practices like walking, praying, and listening to books like *The Surrender Experiment*. These habits helped me decompress and reconnect with the bigger picture. They also reminded me that while I was responsible for putting in the effort, I didn't need to control every outcome. There's a peace that comes with letting go of what you can't control.

Above all, *try to stay calm and trust the process.* Selling a business is inherently stressful, but focusing on your anxiety doesn't help. It only clouds your judgment. Instead, focus on what's in your control. Get the right sell-side advisor (and coach), prepare thoroughly, communicate clearly, and then trust that your efforts will pay off.

STAY FOCUSED ON YOUR GOALS

When offers start rolling in, it's important to recognize the red flags. Try not to get swept up in the excitement of a high offer and start negotiating with yourself. There were a few high-value offers that tempted me to compromise on my *must-haves.* I would think, *Well, maybe staying on for another year or two wouldn't be so bad,* or *Could I make this work if it means hitting that big number?*

But those justifications are a slippery slope. I had to remind myself of my *why.* If I sacrificed my bigger goals for a bigger payout, what was the point of selling in the first place? At times, other offers came in with what looked like impressive valuations but were loaded with contingencies, like extended earnouts, owner financing, or equity rollover. These structures would have tied me to the business for years and undermined the very reasons I was selling.

That's why I encourage you to revisit your written goals frequently—even daily. Fortunately, as you'll recall, I had written out my *must-haves*, my *nice-to-haves*, and the scriptures that grounded me. So when offers came in that conflicted with those priorities, it was easier to step back, take a deep breath, and say no.

Selling your business is one of the most significant decisions you'll ever make. It's a process that tests your patience, your resilience, and your ability to stay true to your values. But if you're clear about your priorities and willing to walk away from offers that don't align, you'll find the right fit.

For me, as I said, the key was staying grounded in my faith, my family, and my vision. It wasn't always easy, and there were moments of doubt. But by focusing on what truly mattered, I was able to make decisions I'm proud of. And that is a success that goes beyond any valuation.

HIROSHI

Pulling into his garage after a delicious dinner with Charles and Alma, Hiroshi was happy. It had been great to see his friends again, and after talking with them, he was more excited than ever to exit his business.

As he walked into the house, he thought about one of the things that Charles had said to him over the meal. The conversation had (rather surprisingly) turned to the importance of having the right mind-set, not to mention faith, to help ensure a successful outcome. Before the conversation moved on to other things, Charles looked him dead in the eye and said, "Looking back, I can see that the calmness I brought to the process, both in mindset and in action, helped me achieve a successful outcome. My advisor and my coach also helped keep me—and the process—steady. Strive to maintain a steady hand through every twist and turn, and it will serve you well in the end."

EIGHT

FAITH AND VISION

ANDY

AITH AND VISION PLAY A FUNDAMENTAL ROLE IN
entrepreneurship, but they aren't often discussed in traditional business books. Most entrepreneurs focus on strategy,
execution, and financials. These are all critical components,
no doubt, but *belief* in the outcome is just as important.

*When you're navigating the challenges of running or
selling a business, faith—whether in a higher power,
in yourself, or in the process—can make the difference
between pushing forward and giving up.*

For Jonathan, faith was a guiding force throughout his
entrepreneurial journey, not to mention his life. We were well

aligned in that regard, as I also take a faith-based approach to leadership and life. The reality is, when you plan for the future—whether it's an annual business strategy or a long-term exit plan—you're making projections based on assumptions. Markets shift, unexpected challenges arise, and obstacles you never saw coming can derail your best-laid plans. Faith, in whatever form, provides the foundation to keep moving forward, knowing that even in uncertainty, progress is possible.

I've seen this firsthand over and over again. For example, I'm currently working with another client, a business owner with a strong Jewish faith who recently hit an unexpected roadblock in the sale of his company. The situation was largely out of his hands, and there was not much my firm or his advisors could do to change the circumstances. Yet instead of panicking, he leaned into his faith, taking the process one step at a time, tackling what he could each day and trusting that he would come out the other side.

His ability to stay grounded despite the unknowns gave him the resilience to push through. I have no doubt we'll successfully complete the sale, but more importantly, his belief in the process is what will carry him through the difficult times.

TRUST THE PROCESS

For entrepreneurs preparing to sell their business, faith is often intertwined with trust. They need to trust their advisors, their team, and the sale process itself. Selling a company is more than merely a transaction. It's a strategic process and journey that requires skill, patience, and confidence in the professionals guiding you through it.

A successful exit depends on a strong relationship between the seller and their sell-side advisor. The seller must trust that their advisor is representing their best interests, while the advisor must trust that the seller is forthcoming and transparent about the business's strengths and weaknesses. Without that mutual trust, the process becomes fractured and uncertain.

When we run a strategic process, we don't just match sellers with buyers based on market expectations. There's an art to it—we are matchmakers, positioning the company in a way that attracts strategic buyers who see more value in the business than just financials. As an example, the market might dictate an average valuation of 8x EBITDA, but a strategic buyer might see the business as transformative and be willing to pay twice that amount because of the potential synergies.

For business owners who lead with faith, alignment with their advisors is also important. That doesn't mean their advisor has to share their religious beliefs, but there should be a shared value system and ethical foundation that makes the working relationship strong. When there is alignment in principles, it helps keep both sides grounded, even when challenges arise.

RECOGNIZE MARKETING TACTICS VS. TRUE EXPERTISE

As part of building trust, business owners looking for a sell-side advisor should also be on the lookout for how prospective advisors present themselves. Many firms rely on aggressive marketing tactics: hosting free exit-planning seminars, sending out mass emails claiming expertise in business sales, or touting they have a buyer interested in your business. While some of these events, emails, or phone calls might be useful, many are designed as lead-generation tools rather than actual educational resources.

Our firm takes a different approach. We don't rely on cold outreach, mass marketing, or generic exit seminars. Every deal we take on comes from referrals and trusted channel partners. This means that by the time we start working with a business owner, there is already a foundation of trust. That level of credibility matters because selling a business is one of the most significant decisions an entrepreneur will ever make.

All of our managing directors are former CEOs and business owners who have firsthand experience with leading companies, both on a daily basis and through mergers and acquisitions. I ran manufacturing businesses myself, so when I worked with Jonathan, I understood the challenges he faced daily—both in operations and in managing his team. That experience allowed me to approach the sale of his business with a perspective that went beyond just a financial transaction.

Our directors come from similar backgrounds, but with different expertise. As former CFOs with strong M&A experience, our financial experts can communicate with a seller's CFO and the buyer's finance team at a peer-to-peer level. That dynamic makes a significant difference. When I engage with a buyer's CEO or division leader, I speak from experience because I've been in their shoes. This isn't just another deal to us. It's about finding the right strategic fit for both the buyer and the seller, ensuring long-term success for both parties.

Buyers recognize that distinction. It builds credibility and increases their trust in the process, knowing they aren't just dealing with "transactional" investment bankers looking to close another deal. That trust also translates into higher valuations because when a buyer believes in the strategic value of a business, they are often willing to pay a premium. In some cases, they may even need the acquisition to meet their own growth goals, making it a *must-have* rather than a *nice-to-have*.

Finding the right sell-side advisor, legal counsel, and financial experts is critical for a smooth exit. Among *many* other things, a strong advisor will:

- Connect sellers with reputable accountants for the quality of earnings (QofE) review
- Recommend experienced M&A attorneys who specialize in business sales

- Refer sellers to great financial advisors, tax advisors, and estate planning advisors to optimize wealth preservation from the exit
- Ensure buyers recognize the business as well prepared and professionally represented
- Strive to develop, understand, and communicate the strategic value of the combined business (the seller's with the buyer's)

Many entrepreneurs don't have deep networks in M&A and might not know which firms are reputable. Buyers, on the other hand, do know the key players, and seeing a well-respected firm handling the transaction gives them faith and confidence in the seller's seriousness and professionalism, not to mention that the transaction will be brought to a successful close.

Ultimately, selling a business is a complex, emotionally charged process that requires both financial rigor and strategic advisory. The most successful transactions are driven by:

- Early financial, operational, and organizational preparation
- Strong sell-side advisors who can manage the emotional and strategic complexities of the sale
- A well-structured competitive process that ensures both buyers and sellers remain aligned from start to finish to achieve a great strategic fit

- Faith and trust in the process, the advisor, and/or a higher power

The right preparation coupled with the right mindset not only increases valuation and deal certainty but also makes the entire process smoother and less stressful. Entrepreneurs who take these steps set themselves up for an optimal exit—one that reflects the true value of what they've built.

ALMA

To her friends and family, Alma didn't always seem like a self-reflective person. However, she had been thinking a lot about her exit in the months after the sale. Lately, she had come to the conclusion that one of the biggest mistakes she made was not getting her mindset right before starting the process.

She had gone into it with a rather vague sense of dissatisfaction with her business—one that drove her to think about selling without getting clear on her *why*. On top of that, she was busy running the business, so she didn't have time to get as prepared as she should have before the sale process started. And, maybe worst of all, she didn't focus on hiring a dedicated sell-side advisor that she trusted—instead, she had chosen someone who reached out to her with the claim that they had a buyer interested in a business like hers. That didn't turn out to be exactly true, which rattled her confidence and left her second-guessing her decision to hire him.

Shaking her head, she thought about how much better her outcome might have been if she had made different choices. She hoped Hiroshi had listened to her words of caution when they last had dinner and avoided making the same mistakes she had.

NAVIGATING "INTEREST"

JONATHAN

W HEN WE STARTED THE SALE PROCESS, WE
expected to receive a few indications of interest
(IOIs) from potential buyers, but nothing quite prepared me for the range of offers and emotions that
would come with them. Over the course of two weeks,
from March 10 to March 24, we received seven formal IOIs.
There may have been others that were so far off the mark that
they never made it to my desk, but the ones I reviewed represented a broad spectrum of interest levels and valuations.

The initial IOIs varied widely in their offers for the company, with the highest anywhere from 2x–4x greater than
the lowest. The buyer who ultimately acquired our company initially submitted an IOI that was in the middle of the

pack—and far lower than what we ultimately agreed on. One IOI came in well above that initial offer, but it required a significant rollover, meaning a significant portion of the sale proceeds would be tied up in the future performance of the company. That wasn't what I wanted. Others had aggressive earnout structures, meaning I'd have to stay involved in the business and hit specific performance milestones to receive the full payout. Some were so restrictive that, despite the attractive headline numbers, they weren't truly viable.

This stage of the process was both exciting and exhausting. Offers were coming in, which was validating, but I also started to feel the weight of decision-making. One thing that helped me navigate this was setting a bottom line. This reflected my minimum required outcome—a number below which I wouldn't sell. This gave me clarity and eliminated the temptation to second-guess myself as offers came in, because it was a number that accounted for both the financial security I wanted *and* the freedom I needed to focus on my family.

ISOLATE THE SERIOUS BUYERS

After reviewing the IOIs, we worked with Andy to filter through the serious players and assess who would be a great home for the business. Some offers were easy to dismiss. They either didn't align with my goals or included unfavorable terms. Others were worth considering.

At this point, emotions were running high. As you know, we had gone into this process months earlier thinking we might sell for a conservative amount. We soon increased that initial target by 50 percent, and now we were seeing offers well beyond that increase. The company had grown, and our profitability had increased.

Once we narrowed down the pool, Andy and his team scheduled in-person management presentations. These were my opportunity to meet the "finalist" buyers in person and sell the company beyond the financials. They also gave us a chance to get potential buyers to believe in our vision by demonstrating our trajectory, our culture, and the opportunity for growth. Last but not least, these meetings afforded the buyers the opportunity to sell *me* on why they were the best home for my business, not to mention the best fit when it came to fulfilling all the outcomes. We had separate meetings with four serious buyers, sitting down in a hotel conference room in Atlanta (to maintain confidentiality, we decided not to hold the meetings in the small town where our company was located) with customized presentations tailored for each meeting. These presentations were expansions of the CIM—customized to each buyer, they addressed their unique questions and highlighted the value points each of the buyers identified through due diligence.

I knew these meetings could be a defining moment, so I worked with a professional communications coach that Andy recommended to refine my delivery. We rehearsed my presentation multiple times, ensuring I could confidently walk potential buyers through every detail of the business. Some meetings were highly engaging, with buyers asking insightful questions and showing real enthusiasm. Others were more reserved, with minimal interaction, which made it harder to gauge their interest.

One buyer stood out—the one we ultimately chose. The CEO was so energized that before I even finished my presentation, he stood up and signaled he was ready to move forward. That was the kind of confidence and excitement I wanted to see—it was clear to both of us that we had a great strategic fit and opportunity.

MOVE TO THE NEXT PHASE

The next step in the process was moving to the letter of intent (LOI) and due diligence phase. This is where the deal takes its final shape, and the buyer and seller begin the intricate process of structuring the transition. Understanding how to manage this phase effectively can mean the difference between a deal closing successfully—or having it fall apart.

After the management presentations, we received four final LOIs—two from strategic buyers and two from financial (private equity) firms. The PE firms had strong offers, but they required us to roll over a portion of our equity, meaning I'd still be financially tied to the company post-sale. That option had its benefits, potentially earning more money down the road, but it also meant staying involved in the business until they could find a new leader.

The strategic buyers, on the other hand, offered full cash-out options and didn't need me to stay on as the day-to-day leader, which aligned with my initial goal of exiting completely. One of the strategic buyers was already a supplier to other businesses in the industry of the same raw materials we used, which created natural synergies that could drive additional value for both businesses beyond the transaction itself. They also had a national footprint, so they could readily duplicate our manufacturing model and expand across the United States.

When we made our final decision, we went back to the *must-have* list we created at the beginning of the process. Did this offer meet my nonnegotiables? Yes. Even though it wasn't the highest offer, the strategic buyer checked every box: a full cash-out, strong cultural alignment, and a vision for the company that I believed in. I took time to think it over, but ultimately, the choice was clear.

Looking back, the process was intense, but by staying focused on my priorities, I walked away with a deal that exceeded my expectations, both financially and strategically.

SELL YOURSELF (AND YOUR TEAM)

Remember, when you're selling a company, you're also selling *yourself*—your competence, your leadership, the great team *you've* built, and your ability to navigate tough conversations. Whether you're staying on board or stepping away, the buyers need to trust that you're the kind of person who can articulate complex ideas, manage relationships, and ensure a smooth transition.

Throughout the sale process, I was very aware of this dynamic. I treated every meeting, whether it was a formal board meeting, a presentation, or a due diligence session, like a pitch. I had spent years in sales and working with customers, so I understood the importance of presentation and preparation. You don't have to be a polished public speaker, but you do need to project confidence and authenticity. That starts with the basics: dressing appropriately (not over the top, but put-together), knowing your numbers inside and out, and making sure you've internalized key talking points so the conversation feels natural.

I went into these meetings prepared, not just because I wanted to make a good impression, but because I knew *no one else could sell my business better than me*. Of course, my sell-side advisor team was there to support and guide me, but when it came down to answering critical questions, the buyers wanted to hear it directly from me. They needed to see that I was competent, that I could explain the strategy and operations clearly, and that I had built something solid.

For entrepreneurs considering an exit, this is a key piece of advice. *You need to be involved in the process.* You can't just hand everything over to an advisor and hope for the best. Buyers want to know they're dealing with someone who understands every aspect of their business, who has thought through the future, and who can communicate effectively.

Even if you're not staying on post-sale, the ability to navigate these conversations matters. And if you are, they become especially important. After all, if you will have any level of involvement in the business after the sale, you need to show that you're someone they can work with—someone they like, trust, and respect.

MAINTAIN GROWTH THROUGH THE SALE PROCESS

One of the biggest challenges during an acquisition is keeping the business on track and stable (or growing) while juggling the demands of the sale. Buyers want to see a thriving business, not one that's losing momentum as the owner gets distracted.

Fortunately, I had already built a leadership structure that ensured the business could run without me. A year prior to the sale, I had shifted my focus toward empowering my leadership team, ensuring that day-to-day operations wouldn't grind to a halt if I wasn't involved in every decision. This meant:

- Hiring strong leaders and ensuring they had autonomy over their departments
- Developing a second layer of leadership so that no single person (including me) was indispensable
- Keeping a relentless focus on sales and growth, even as we worked through the sale process

I never took my foot off the gas when it came to growth. We maintained our sales momentum, which was important because our projections and financials were based on a growing company. I wanted to make it clear to the buyer that by the time the deal closed, this business would be bigger and more valuable than when the process started. And it was: We handed the buyer a very strong order backlog for their stability and growth.

This is a key point. If we had fallen short on our numbers, the deal still might have happened, but we wouldn't have gotten a strategic premium. After all, buyers don't just look at historical performance—they want to see a company that's still on an upward trajectory.

For anyone preparing to sell their business, this is non-negotiable. The best way to ensure a smooth exit, maximize valuation, and retain leverage in negotiations is to keep the company growing, even when your focus is being pulled in a hundred different directions.

This brings us back to the idea of *founder risk*. One of the most common mistakes entrepreneurs make is building a business that is entirely dependent on them. They are the rainmakers, the problem-solvers, the ones making key decisions every day. That works fine until they decide they want to sell. Suddenly, buyers aren't just looking at financials; they're evaluating the business's sustainability. If your company can't function without you, then what exactly are buyers purchasing?

I knew early on that I needed to build a company that could run without me. Whether I sold the business or not, I didn't want to be the bottleneck. So I focused on hiring strong leaders—someone to oversee operations, someone to handle finance, and someone to drive sales. Even if I had never sold the business, this structure was important for growth. Without it, I would have worked myself into the ground.

Building a strong leadership team is one of the best things you can do, both for the long-term success of your business and for increasing its value to potential buyers. This isn't just about the top-tier executives, either. Buyers want to see strength at multiple levels, including mid-level managers who truly own their departments. In my case, we were a manufacturing-heavy operation, so having a solid operations team was critical.

When I started looking at what it would take to allow the business to operate without me, I asked myself a few questions:

- What decisions am I still making that I shouldn't be?
- What problems keep coming back to me instead of being solved elsewhere?
- If I disappeared tomorrow, what gaps would be left behind?

The answers to these questions helped me identify the weaknesses in my organizational structure. I suggest you ask yourself the same things, because if you're constantly the one answering operational questions, troubleshooting problems, or handling customer relationships, then you haven't built a company that most buyers are willing to pay a premium for.

For many entrepreneurs, letting go of control is the hardest part. If you've spent years growing a business, chances are you're great in a specific functional area of your company. Maybe it's sales, maybe it's product development, maybe it's operations. Whatever it is, that expertise often becomes part of your identity. Handing it off to someone else feels risky.

I struggled with this myself. I knew I needed to step back, but I told myself, "Nobody can do this as well as I can." I was convinced that my expertise in sales was irreplaceable. Sure, I could delegate other tasks, but closing deals with high-end clients? Handling key accounts? That had to be me.

That mindset is a trap. The truth is, if you want your business to scale, and if you want to eventually sell it, you have to be okay with someone else doing things 80 percent as well as you would. Maybe they won't be as sharp in negotiations. Maybe they won't close deals quite as smoothly. But if they can do it well enough to keep the business moving forward, that's a win.

Another big obstacle entrepreneurs face is the time it takes to train someone. It's easy to think, *I should delegate this, but it would take so much time to train someone that it's easier to just do it myself.* That's one of the biggest lies we tell ourselves. If you want to have a successful exit, you must put in the hard work of training people, even when it feels like a time drain. Yes, they will make mistakes at first. Yes, it will take longer than just doing it yourself. But once they are fully up to speed, you will have freed yourself from the day-to-day operations, which makes the business far more attractive to a buyer.

START PREPARING EARLY

Many entrepreneurs wait to start preparing for a sale until just a few months before they put the business on the market. However, as I'm sure you realize by now, if you wait until the last minute to build a leadership team, put systems in place, and remove yourself from the business, you'll find yourself in an incredibly stressful situation. You might still sell, but you won't get the best price or the best terms. Buyers will see the lack of infrastructure and either walk away or demand heavy earnouts to ensure the business doesn't collapse the moment you step away.

These principles apply no matter how much EBITDA the business is making. *Buyers want to acquire a system, not a personality-driven business.* If you're the one holding everything together, that's a risk for them.

A business that depends on its owner to function is like a house held together with duct tape and zip ties. It might still be standing, but a buyer will see the underlying problems. If you know that some part of your operation is barely holding on, fix it before you sell—not after a buyer discovers it during due diligence.

Ultimately, if you want to build a company that buyers will pay a premium for, put yourself in the buyer's shoes. Ask yourself:

- *Would I want to buy this company if I knew everything about it?*
- *What risks might scare me away?*
- *What would make me feel confident that this business can run and grow without the current owner?*

At the end of the day, the best way to sell a business is to build one that doesn't need you. That means setting up the right culture, leaders, and systems; letting go of control; and preparing long before you think you're ready. It's a difficult shift, but it's also the key to a successful and profitable exit.

MASTER PREPARATION AND BALANCE

Even if you're years away from selling, it's never too early to start preparing. Document your standard operating procedures. Diversify your revenue streams. Eliminate red flags like compliance issues or bad debts. By taking these steps, you create a business that can function optimally on a daily basis without your oversight—which is exactly what buyers want.

We took the time to do all of that, correctly and from the beginning. And, as I discussed earlier, it paid off even more handsomely than I initially expected. Andy's team framed what we had done as a major competitive advantage for buyers who value businesses with robust processes over people-dependent operations.

Diversity in revenue streams was another strength Andy's team zeroed in on. My business served commercial, residential, storage, agricultural, and roofing markets, which created stability across seasons and economic cycles. "Buyers are all about minimizing risk," Andy told me. "The more diverse and stable your revenue, the more valuable your business."

He was exactly right, and he parlayed that knowledge into a higher valuation for my company.

ALMA AND HIROSHI

"Thanks for meeting with me, Alma," Hiroshi said as they waited for the hostess to show them to their table. "I had lunch with Charles a week or so ago, and he gave me a lot of great advice. I'm getting closer to getting the ball rolling on hiring a dedicated sell-side advisor to help me sell my business, but I wanted to talk to you a bit more about your experience before I do."

"It's my pleasure, Hiroshi!" said Alma. "Anything I can do to help make sure you have the best exit possible."

As the hostess led them to their table, Hiroshi told Alma he had been wondering how important it was to maintain growth during the sale process. "After all, it could take nine months or more to actually sell, right? My business is in a good place, and I know that I'll have to devote a lot of time and attention to selling. Is it okay if we just remain stable?"

"I guess it's okay," Alma replied, "but in my experience, it's not ideal. The most important thing is for a business to have historic growth *and* solid projections for future growth. I've been thinking about this a lot, and I realized that when I took my foot off the gas a bit during the sale process, it negatively impacted the final offer. Making a point of maintaining growth will make your business even more attractive to the buyer, and the more attractive it is, the better your outcome will be."

"Look," she continued. "I know that you've worked hard to make your business recession-proof, but put yourself in the buyer's shoes. Would *you* want to buy a business that doesn't show strong growth—no matter the reason? Or would you worry about the risks that you might acquire something that won't scale the way you hoped? I know it's not easy, but that's why it's so great that you're taking steps to prepare now, well before your business is actually for sale: You'll be able to confidently demonstrate to buyers that your company can keep growing and scaling even when your attention is on something other than the day-to-day operations. I wish I had done that, but at least you can learn from my mistake."

"That makes sense," Hiroshi said. "For the most part, my business has solid systems and automations in place to make growth easy, but there are a few holes. I know my attention is going to be pulled in a lot of different directions, so I'll start taking steps now to make sure that my team and my processes are set up to achieve scalability and growth, no matter what happens."

NAVIGATING DUE DILIGENCE

ANDY

FTER THE LOI STAGE, IT'S TIME FOR DUE diligence. Due diligence is a critical phase in any merger or acquisition, where the buyer conducts an exhaustive review of the business they intend to purchase. This process involves assessing every aspect of the company's operations, risks, and growth potential (and I do mean *every* aspect). Buyers want to uncover any hidden liabilities and risks, ensure that what they see on paper aligns with reality, and validate that there's integrated strategic value between what they and the company bring to the table.

While doing an exhaustive dive into due diligence is beyond the scope of this book, it's worth taking the time here to talk about some of the most important parts of this process.

One key area of due diligence is *financial verification*, where buyers analyze financial statements, revenue streams, and overall profitability to ensure accuracy and integrity. Even if your company's financials have been audited, the buyer—usually with the assistance of a third-party accounting firm—will conduct a quality of earnings (QofE) assessment to validate the numbers and identify any red flags. I strongly suggest you hire a third-party accounting firm to conduct a sell-side QofE in advance, to be more prepared for the buyer's financial due diligence, and to streamline the entire financial diligence process.

COMPLETE A SELL-SIDE QUALITY OF EARNINGS REPORT

A QofE is a financial due diligence review that is carried out by an independent third-party accounting firm and is designed to validate and normalize your company's financials. While many buyers conduct their own QofE analysis before acquiring a business, my team and I strongly recommend that sellers proactively complete one beforehand to be better prepared for the buyer's due diligence.

A QofE report examines financial statements to assess the quality of revenue, cash flow, earnings, and working capital. It helps identify one-time, nonrecurring expenses and adjustments that should be excluded from the financials (as "add-backs"), ultimately presenting a clearer and often stronger picture of profitability. For example, if a company recently implemented a new ERP system at a one-time cost of $200,000, that expense would be classified as an "add-back" since it does not recur annually. So, the profit of the company would be normalized to be $200,000 better in that year. Similarly, if the company incurred temporary costs related to preparing for the sale, such as legal fees or consulting expenses, those can also be adjusted.

Beyond add-backs, a QofE helps normalize financials to reflect the true earning potential of a business. This includes:

- **New Expenses That Haven't Been Fully Realized**: If a company recently hired a high-salaried executive but has only incurred three months of expenses so far, the QofE will reflect the full annual cost to provide an accurate projection to the buyer.

- **New Revenue Streams**: If a business recently signed a multiyear contract but has recorded only two months of revenue, the QofE can annualize the revenue and profit impact by adding a full pro forma twelve-month run rate of that revenue and profit to provide a more realistic view of annualized future earnings.

- **Cost-Saving Measures**: If a company has implemented operational efficiencies or supplier cost reductions that will result in ongoing savings, the QofE can reflect those improvements on a pro forma basis.

This process is not an audit but rather a deep forensic financial validation. It ensures that the numbers a seller presents to buyers are accurate, justifiable, and transparent, especially with adjustments that improve performance beyond the financial statements. Having a third-party firm validate these numbers adds credibility, preventing buyers from attempting to negotiate a lower price based on financial uncertainties.

There are several major benefits to having a QofE report completed *before* going to market:

1. **Preparedness for Buyer Due Diligence:** When buyers conduct their own due diligence, sellers who have already been through the process are better equipped to answer questions and provide documentation. This streamlines negotiations and reduces the risk of surprises that could delay or derail a deal. In some cases, a buyer may not do a QofE if the sell-side QofE is sufficient for their internal due diligence team.

2. **Stronger Valuations:** By identifying legitimate financial adjustments, a QofE can increase reported EBITDA to normalized, adjusted EBITDA—and

justify a higher valuation. For example, if a business reports $10 million in EBITDA but has $700,000 in one-time expenses and other adjustments that should be added back, the true EBITDA could be closer to $10.7 million. With a multiple of 8x, that $700,000 adjustment could translate to an additional $5.6 million in valuation.

3. **Building Buyer Confidence:** Buyers take sellers more seriously when they present a well-documented financial package. A QofE signals that the business is professionally managed and prepared for sale, reducing perceived risk for the buyer.

4. **Defensive Protection Against Buyer Negotiation Tactics:** Some buyers intentionally challenge a company's reported financials and EBITDA, arguing that actual earnings are lower than presented. Without a QofE, a seller may struggle to refute these claims. However, when a third-party firm has already validated the financials, it becomes much harder for buyers to push for a lower valuation.

A QofE typically takes six to eight weeks to complete, and while costs can range from $50,000 to $100,000 or more, the return on investment is often significant. If it helps increase the company's EBITDA by even a fraction, it easily justifies the cost, many times over.

Ultimately, a QofE report is an investment in the sale process. It reduces friction, builds credibility, and helps maximize value for the seller. By demonstrating a commitment to financial transparency and professionalism, it sets the stage for a smoother transaction with fewer surprises and stronger negotiating leverage.

Once buyers enter the picture, the QofE report becomes a key tool in the negotiation process. It provides a detailed financial overview that answers many of the questions buyers would ask before they even ask them. Some buyers—especially those with strong internal finance teams—will forgo hiring a third-party firm for due diligence and instead rely heavily on the seller's QofE report. Others will conduct their own due diligence but will use the seller's QofE as a baseline for validation.

Having a third-party firm validate earnings and financial adjustments makes it easier for both parties. The seller's third-party accounting team, which conducted the QofE, can directly engage with the buyer's due diligence team to clarify any questions, minimizing disruptions for the seller. This speeds up the process, ensures smoother negotiations, and reduces the likelihood of last-minute valuation disputes where buyers attempt to lower the sale price by challenging financial assumptions.

PREP FOR OTHER TYPES OF DILIGENCE

Alongside financial due diligence, *commercial due diligence*—which focuses on customer relationships, sales trends, and market position—also takes place. During commercial due diligence, buyers evaluate customer churn, whether customers are repeat buyers, if the business offers subscription-based recurring sales models, the cyclicality of the business, and whether revenue is cyclical or too dependent on a few key clients, among other points. In many cases, third-party research firms also assess the company's competitive standing, customer sentiment, and market trends.

Legal and tax due diligence ensures that contracts (particularly those that require assignment or consent in the case of a sale), compliance measures, and tax obligations have been handled correctly. Attorneys review all agreements, including supplier contracts, employment agreements, and customer agreements, to identify potential risks. Tax specialists evaluate payroll compliance, remittances, and outstanding tax liabilities.

Meanwhile, *operational due diligence* focuses on the company's internal processes, systems, procedures, production facilities, and supply chain dependencies. One of the most important things buyers look for here is whether the business relies heavily on a single supplier. If it does, it presents a major risk that buyers must consider. Another key area buyers investigate is whether the business's systems and processes are properly documented, repeatable, and consistently deliver quality to the customer.

Environmental due diligence is another important factor, especially for businesses in manufacturing and energy, as buyers need to confirm there are no hidden environmental liabilities.

Technology and intellectual property (IP) due diligence assesses the company's patents, trademarks, formulations, specialized know-how, and proprietary software. Buyers verify that all IP assets are properly registered and legally protected.

Workforce and organizational due diligence examines employee retention, leadership structure, and company culture, as high turnover rates or cultural issues could indicate deeper operational problems. Perhaps most importantly, buyers consider whether the company has the needed organization to support future growth.

UNDERSTAND HOW THE PROCESS UNFOLDS

Due diligence is typically conducted in phases, beginning with an initial assessment and gradually progressing to a deep-dive analysis. Before submitting an LOI, buyers conduct a preliminary review of performance and trends in key areas of the business, including financial, commercial, human resources, technical, operations, industry, competitors, market position, growth opportunities, and more. This high-level assessment allows them to determine if the business aligns with their investment strategy. At this stage, sellers may redact customer names and other sensitive details to protect confidentiality.

Phases of Due Diligence

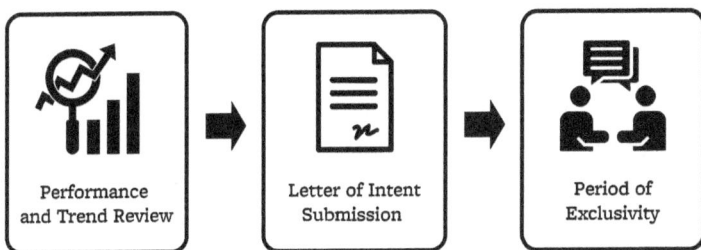

Performance and Trend Review	Letter of Intent Submission	Period of Exclusivity

Once an LOI is submitted, buyers may be granted access to more detailed financials, contracts, and operational data. A virtual data room is often used to store and organize these records, allowing the buyer's team to review everything efficiently. As the process moves forward, buyers conduct deeper due diligence in areas such as finance, legal compliance, operational efficiency, commercial aspects, and areas of strategic value.

The final stage of due diligence is the *exclusivity period*, typically lasting sixty to ninety days. During this stage, which also includes negotiating and finalizing the purchase agreement and other needed agreements (i.e., employment, transition services, and so on), the selected "best" buyer conducts an exhaustive review before finalizing the deal. This phase involves significant financial investment as the buyer brings in third-party firms to support the due diligence process. Total costs to the buyer for this part of the process can range from $300,000 to over $1 million, depending on the size and complexity of a typical middle-market transaction. If no major red flags arise, the deal proceeds to final contract negotiations and closing. However, if due diligence uncovers critical risks, buyers may renegotiate terms, adjust valuation, or even walk away from the deal.

As you can see, due diligence is a complex, resource-intensive process, but it is essential for ensuring that both parties enter the transaction with clear expectations and confidence in the business's long-term viability. For sellers, preparing well in advance by organizing financial records, contracts, succession planning, organizational resources, and compliance documentation can significantly streamline the process and improve the chances of a successful sale.

BE ORGANIZED AND PROACTIVE

The best way for sellers to prepare for diligence is to work with an experienced sell-side advisor who can provide a comprehensive due diligence checklist tailored to their industry. Every transaction is different, and while financial due diligence is universal, areas such as intellectual property and regulatory compliance will vary depending on the industry. For example, the due diligence required for a manufacturing business will differ from that of a SaaS or IT company, so it's in your best interest to work with a seasoned sell-side advisor who understands what buyers in any given industry are looking for.

Advisors typically categorize due diligence requirements into priority levels. *Priority one* items—such as financial statements, customer and supplier historical trends and agreements, employee records, key technology, assets, tax filings, and legal contracts—are critical and required by nearly all buyers. *Priority two* and *priority three* items, while important, may vary depending on the buyer's focus and specific concerns. Regardless of priority level, though, organizing these materials ahead of time helps prevent delays once due diligence begins. A good sell-side advisor will provide a detailed list of all the potential due diligence items, as well as a tracking system to manage the various documents as they are gathered and organized in the virtual data room.

In some cases, sellers may lack the internal resources to manage due diligence efficiently. Hiring a fractional CFO or bringing in a third-party financial consultant can provide the necessary support to gather and organize documents while allowing the business's internal team to focus on day-to-day operations.

Once due diligence officially begins, it becomes a complex back-and-forth between the buyer, the seller, and their respective advisors. To streamline this process, sellers should work with their advisors to establish a virtual data room on a highly secure platform where all required documents can be uploaded in an organized manner. A well-structured data room will typically have dedicated folders for each functional area of the company and the targeted areas of due diligence, such as financials, contracts, customers, suppliers, environmental reports, employee records, intellectual property, tax, information systems, products, and legal, to name a few.

Buyers, especially private equity firms, often have detailed due diligence workbooks: comprehensive checklists covering every function of the business. As they go through their review, they will submit requests for clarification, additional documentation, or supporting data. A good sell-side advisor will act as an intermediary, handling these inquiries and reducing the burden on the seller.

STRUCTURE THE SALE CORRECTLY

As sellers move through the due diligence process, they need to be aware of the different types of deal structures and how they affect both the seller and the buyer. That's because deal structure can impact everything about the sale, including tax implications to the seller and liabilities to the buyer.

At a high level, deals are generally structured as either asset sales or stock sales. In a stock sale, the legal entity remains unchanged, so all contracts remain in place without requiring assignment from the other party. Conversely, in an asset sale, buyers are buying only the assets of the business, and they don't take on any liabilities outside of the balance sheet.

Typically, a stock deal is more tax efficient for the seller, but since it transfers liabilities (i.e., environmental, legal, and so on) to the buyer, most buyers prefer asset deals. However, depending on the business, asset deals aren't always the best way to go. For example, some contracts with customers, vendors, and any other relevant parties include provisions that prevent them from being transferred to a new owner without approval. If the seller has hundreds of such agreements, this can become a logistical challenge. In these cases, structuring the deal as a stock sale rather than an asset sale can simplify the transition. That's because in an asset sale, the contracts must be assigned to the new entity, which requires extensive outreach to customers, vendors, and other parties if consent is required—something most sellers want to avoid before the deal is finalized.

These different deal structures can lead to one of the major challenges of due diligence: contract assignability and change of control. In any deal, whether structured as an asset sale or a stock sale, contracts with customers, vendors, and partners must be reviewed for transferability. A stock sale maintains the legal entity but may require change of control approval, meaning key customers or partners must consent to the new ownership. This can be a deal-breaker if a significant client, especially one that makes up a significant percentage of revenue, refuses (or is at risk of refusing) to do business with the new owner.

If the deal is structured as an asset sale, contracts must be formally assigned or rewritten to the new legal owner entity, which can be even more complex. Sellers must notify customers and vendors about the transition and obtain their approval for assignment. If there are hundreds of contracts, this process can be overwhelming and create risk for the deal. Buyers often prefer asset sales to avoid assuming prior liabilities, but when assignment requirements create roadblocks, parties must consider alternative structures.

There are other considerations to make when determining deal structure. Is there rollover? Earnouts? Seller financing? Cash to close? How much of the business is being sold? And so on.

As you can see, there's a lot to think about—and negotiate— here. That's why sellers should work closely with a seasoned sell-side advisor and M&A attorney to make sure the deal is structured correctly. By anticipating potential challenges, organizing key materials ahead of time, and working closely with experienced advisors, sellers can position themselves for a smoother, faster due diligence process and increase the likelihood of a successful transaction.

ASSESS KEY CHALLENGES AND CONSIDERATIONS

Beyond contracts, another common challenge is financial and tax due diligence. Buyers will scrutinize the company's financial history, looking for inconsistencies or potential liabilities. A major red flag can be undisclosed tax obligations. For example, in one case, a seller we worked with had collected sales tax in multiple states but failed to properly remit those funds. The issue only surfaced during deep due diligence, forcing the seller to self-report and pay back taxes and penalties, and indemnify the buyer of any related liabilities. While this particular case was resolved, it could have derailed the deal entirely.

Environmental due diligence is another potential roadblock. If a company owns or operates facilities on contaminated land or has compliance issues with hazardous materials, a buyer might walk away rather than assume the liability. Some sellers choose to preemptively conduct a Phase One Environmental Review to address potential concerns early, which can be a very smart move. If issues are found, sellers can negotiate a solution, such as setting aside a portion of the sale proceeds for remediation and any related liabilities.

Legal due diligence can also cause deals to unravel. If a company has ongoing lawsuits, unresolved claims, or compliance issues, buyers may demand indemnifications—agreements that make the seller responsible for certain liabilities post-sale. In some cases, buyers will require holdbacks, where a portion of the sale price is withheld in escrow to cover potential future risks. Sellers who are not prepared for these discussions can find themselves blindsided, leading to last-minute disputes that jeopardize the transaction.

AVOIDING DEAL FATIGUE, BURNOUT, AND OTHER PROBLEMS

Beyond the technical challenges, due diligence is often emotionally exhausting. Deal fatigue is real, and it can lead to frustration, poor decision-making, and even the collapse of the entire deal. I've seen it happen time and again: Sellers who are unprepared for the sheer volume of questions and document requests may feel like they are under attack. However, when you are going through diligence, it's important to remember that, in reality, buyers are simply protecting their investment; assessing risks, growth opportunities, and cultural fit; and conducting a standard review.

One of the biggest mistakes I see sellers make is taking due diligence inquiries personally. A buyer's scrutiny is not an attack on the seller's integrity or business acumen—it's a necessary process. Sellers who allow emotions to cloud their judgment may push back on reasonable requests, creating unnecessary tension. In some cases, sellers have walked away from deals simply because they were fed up with the process, even when the deal was financially sound.

Once again, having an experienced team in your corner can make a huge difference to the success of the process. A skilled advisor acts as a buffer, filtering out unnecessary requests, framing responses, managing expectations, and keeping the process on track. On top of that, your coach and, in some cases, even your M&A attorney can also help you remain objective so the deal doesn't break down unnecessarily. Without these intermediaries, deals are far more likely to run into problems due to miscommunication or frustration.

That said, one factor that can stall or kill a deal is legal over-complication. While attorneys play a critical role in protecting their clients, some legal teams focus excessively on minor details, causing unnecessary delays. If left unchecked, attorneys on both sides can engage in drawn-out negotiations over immaterial clauses, driving up costs and extending due diligence beyond reasonable time frames. A strong advisor can step in and push for resolution so that legal teams focus on material risks rather than getting stuck in the weeds.

I've also seen situations where a lawyer is out to "win" an argument to show that their firm is better than the other party's firm, even though that "win" has minimal impact on the deal. In these cases, lawyers let their personal egos get in the way of successfully completing the transaction on behalf of the client, causing headaches and worse for everyone involved.

Sellers should also be prepared for changing deal terms. Buyers may adjust their offer based on due diligence findings, especially if new risks are uncovered. For example, if a company's growth trajectory is less certain than initially believed, a buyer may propose shifting part of the purchase price into an earnout, tying future payments to performance targets. Sellers must decide whether to accept these revised terms or walk away—another area where having an advisor is crucial.

Even for well-prepared sellers, due diligence can be a marathon, not a sprint. Deals can stretch over many months, and the constant back-and-forth with buyers can create the deal fatigue I mentioned earlier—where sellers simply become exhausted with the process and start making hasty decisions just to get it over with. A great sell-side advisor helps maintain momentum while ensuring that the seller doesn't settle for less than they deserve.

Ultimately, though, preparation is the best way to reduce surprises and stress in due diligence. By organizing financial records, reviewing contracts for assignability or consent, addressing potential legal and tax concerns early, and maintaining a level-headed approach, sellers can make due diligence as smooth as possible. While the process is demanding, those who go in with the right mindset and a strong support system will have a far better chance of successfully closing the deal.

CHARLES AND HIROSHI

Charles was loving the extra time that selling his business had afforded him. Along with being able to travel with his family, he also had more time to see his friends. In fact, he and Hiroshi had taken to having lunch as often as possible whenever Charles was in town. As they were wrapping up a meal at a restaurant they both enjoyed, a few months after Charles's exit, he looked at Hiroshi and said, "Remember how I told you a while back that having a strong, experienced, dedicated team is crucial to exiting successfully?"

Hiroshi nodded.

"Well," Charles said, "I just realized that I didn't say anything about the diligence process."

"I've heard from some people that it's tough—mentally draining and emotionally taxing," said Hiroshi.

"It can be," Charles replied. "But a good team will help you through it—and I know you're in the process of building that team for yourself. On top of that, I strongly suggest that you start preparing for diligence well in advance to ease the burden when you get to that stage."

"How?" Hiroshi asked.

"Again, your advisor will help you," Charles said, "but you can speed the process along by organizing your financial records, contracts, succession planning, organizational resources, and compliance documentation. I also suggest working with your sell-side advisor to hire a third-party accounting firm to do a quality of earnings analysis. Taking the time to do all of this can significantly streamline the process and improve your chances of making a successful sale."

Hiroshi smiled. "I'm on it!"

ELEVEN

GETTING YOUR FINANCIALS IN ORDER

JONATHAN

A S WE STARTED TO PREPARE FOR DILIGENCE, Andy's team dug deep to uncover any potential red flags before buyers could. From compliance issues to customer disputes, they left no stone unturned. "Buyers are looking for any signs of shade or sloppiness," Andy told me. Their thoroughness gave me confidence that we'd be ready for anything during due diligence.

Due diligence, as you now know, is the phase where buyers verify every claim you've made and ensure there are no hidden surprises. It's not for the faint of heart. Here, too, having someone in my corner proved invaluable. My coach reminded me to keep my team motivated and the business growing throughout this stage. It's easy to get consumed by the sale process, but letting the business slip during this time can derail everything. However, if you've been careful to prepare for the sale well in advance, the due diligence process will go a lot more smoothly.

If I could give one piece of advice to entrepreneurs considering selling their business, it would be this: Start preparing today.

Even small businesses can benefit from this mindset. While the expectations might differ for smaller operations, the principles of preparation apply universally. Build systems, create clear roles, and document all of your processes. The work you do now will make your business more valuable and easier to manage in the meantime.

BUILD CONFIDENCE FOR DUE DILIGENCE

One of the first major steps I took to prepare for diligence was ensuring our financials were in order. During one of my first meetings with my coach and Andy, they strongly recommended that I commission a quality of earnings (QofE) report. This needed to be conducted by an independent third-party accounting firm for obvious reasons—it's essentially forensic financial due diligence similar to what a buyer will do, with a focus on verifying the financial health and pro forma normalizations of the company in preparation for a sale. It was an incredibly helpful suggestion: A third-party firm conducts financial due diligence the way a buyer will, so you're more prepared for the actual buyer's due diligence process.

We needed a thorough financial assessment, and while my own CPA firm may have been equipped to handle it, they would have been conflicted reviewing their prior work. Andy recommended a reputable, middle-market-focused firm in Atlanta that specialized in this kind of work, and they turned out to be a great choice—reasonable in cost and efficient in execution.

The team came to our office and spent a total of four days combing through our financials. Since we hadn't yet informed any employees about the sale, we had to be discreet. My finance department was told we were conducting an audit, which wasn't untrue—just not the full story. Fortunately, finance professionals understand the audit process, so they didn't question it too much. We needed them to pull detailed financial data and provide accurate reports to the QofE team, and they handled it well.

For any business owner considering a sale, I highly recommend you start conducting annual audits or reviews a couple of years in advance of a sale, especially if your company is young (this isn't required, of course, but it will certainly help when you enter the sale process). At the time, my business was only three and a half years old, so we were still in a phase of rapid growth. I had always intended to start doing annual audits once we were big enough, and had we not been preparing for a sale, that would've been the year we began. Not only do regular audits put you ahead of the game when it comes time for the QofE, but they *also* hold everyone accountable and ensure transparency—both of which are critical if your company has financial leverage with a bank, because lenders want to see clean financials.

Once the QofE team completed their initial on-site work, they continued refining the report from their office. This process took several weeks to complete. Then, each month as we closed our books, the QofE team updated their report, tracking our financial performance right up to the sale. This was important because buyers care deeply about a company's performance in the months leading up to closing. Deals often hinge on those final numbers, and poor financials can cause a deal to be re-traded (reducing the price the buyer is willing to pay) or, even worse, to fall apart at the last minute.

DEALING WITH TENSIONS DURING A SALE

The QofE process was one of the first major actions we took after deciding to sell. My finance department consisted of a director of finance and a bookkeeper, both of whom played important roles in keeping the business running smoothly. My director of finance was particularly skilled with systems and ERP management and had a strong capacity to handle the demands of our fast-growing business. As we scaled, we also hired a bookkeeper that the director had worked with previously, which initially seemed like a great fit.

However, as the company grew and new leadership roles were introduced, tensions arose within the finance team. Rapid growth brings challenges, and not everyone adapts well to a constantly evolving business. When we were small, team members had to wear multiple hats. For example, my director of finance helped not only with finance, but also with sales and operations. As we grew, though, those responsibilities had to be redistributed.

When I brought in a director of operations, it created a power struggle. The finance director and operations director clashed, leading to internal friction. The combination of these conflicts was creating an unhealthy environment.

Eventually, the situation came to a head. My director of finance handed in her resignation, giving me three weeks to find a replacement. It was a nightmare scenario. Not only were we in the midst of finalizing our QofE report, but we were also preparing to sell the company. Finding a qualified finance leader under normal circumstances is challenging, but doing so in a post-pandemic environment amid a business sale was overwhelming.

Realizing the urgency, I turned to my coach, who recommended an outsourced CFO firm. We quickly brought in a team from that firm that included a finance manager and bookkeepers to stabilize our financial operations. They spent a few days on-site working with my outgoing director of finance, then transitioned to running things remotely.

Just when I thought we had things under control, the book-keeper—who had been working under my director of finance—also resigned, citing personal reasons. Suddenly, we were about to lose our entire finance department in the middle of a sale.

To keep things moving, we had the outsourced CFO team step in and take over all financial functions, including payroll, accounts receivable, and accounts payable. At the same time, we launched an aggressive search for an in-house finance director. Selling a business without a stable finance department is a massive red flag for buyers, and I wasn't about to let that happen.

This period of transition was one of the most stressful times in my entrepreneurial journey. It reinforced the importance of building a resilient financial infrastructure well before considering a sale. If I had to do it over again, I would have started annual audits sooner and built a finance team that could withstand internal shifts (and, ideally, had been through a sale process before).

For business owners thinking about selling, another piece of advice I can offer is this: *Get your financial house in order early*. A strong, transparent financial foundation will not only make your company more attractive to buyers, but will also prevent last-minute crises that could jeopardize the deal. *Remember, buyers want to know that your business is stable, sustainable, and ready for the next chapter.*

WALK THE FINE LINE OF TRANSPARENCY

Selling a business comes with its fair share of challenges, and one of the biggest hurdles we faced was maintaining financial stability while navigating the transition. A key function of any business—finance—was in flux, and we had to find a way to manage it without derailing the sale.

Because we had lost key members of our finance team, our financial reporting and projections—critical elements for potential buyers—were suddenly in question. We quickly realized that without a CFO, we needed an interim solution. So, along with the outsourced team, we also brought in a temporary placement in-house to keep things moving. Unfortunately, though, he wasn't the right fit...and ultimately, that situation cost us valuable time.

Meanwhile, we still had to manage the financials for the sale process. Buyers don't just look at a company's earnings—they want to see financial projections that support the business's future. While an accounting team focuses on the day-to-day finance functions that keep the business running, buyers are looking for forward-looking financials that show the company's potential.

Without an internal CFO, we had to rely on an outside party. So, we hired a seasoned fractional CFO (from the same outsourced accounting company we brought on to handle the daily finance function of the business) to prepare the necessary financial reports. His main focus was to get the business's financials in order for the sale. It was a good decision: He stayed with us through the sale process and even attended management presentations in Atlanta to provide clarity on the financial side of the business. Additionally, Andy and his team supported building out the forecast with the information we provided; they worked closely with the outsourced CFO on key assumptions and realistic projections.

At this point, the road split into multiple directions. There was the immediate need to keep financial operations steady, but there was also the long-term need to fill the director of finance role permanently. However, hiring someone full-time wasn't an overnight process. It took months, and by the time we found the right candidate, his first day on the job was just three days before we closed the sale.

This might have been a deal-breaker for some buyers, but in today's world of outsourcing and remote work, it wasn't an insurmountable issue for us. We were up front with the buyer about our finance department situation, and they saw that the business was running smoothly despite the transition. They were receiving financial reports every month, and everything looked solid.

The moral of the story here: Rather than hiding our challenges, *we decided to turn transparency into an advantage.* (Of course, for liability reasons, not to mention integrity, sellers *must* be transparent. Under no circumstances should you mislead the buyer or misrepresent your company.) We let the buyers interview the incoming CFO candidate so they could be part of the solution. This helped build their confidence and made them feel like they had a say in shaping the future leadership of the company.

One of the trickiest aspects of selling a business is keeping buyers informed without overwhelming them with unnecessary details. You want to be honest, but you don't want to project panic. If you come across as chaotic or disorganized, it raises red flags. At the same time, if you downplay issues too much, you risk losing credibility.

The goal is to communicate that you have things under control (which we did, although it was admittedly a very dynamic situation). If a key function is in transition—like our finance department was—buyers will want to know how you're handling it. However, instead of bombarding them with the drama of failed hires or internal struggles, present them with a solution. Assure them that processes are in place, that things are stable, and that the business is operating smoothly despite the temporary gaps.

Bear in mind, our finance team had no idea we were selling. Their departure had nothing to do with the sale. It was just part of the inevitable growing pains of a business in a high-growth phase. But in the end, we adapted, problem-solved, and got the deal done.

Selling a business is never *completely* smooth sailing, but if you approach challenges strategically, communicate wisely, and involve buyers in solutions rather than just problems, you can turn potential obstacles into moments of trust-building.

CHARLES AND HIROSHI

"Tell me a little more about getting ready for diligence in advance," Hiroshi said to Charles, reaching for the check the waiter had just brought.

"Well, again, your advisor will be able to walk you through what you need to do for your specific situation. But I will tell you that I spoke with Alma recently, and she told me she had assumed she could take care of everything once they entered diligence," said Charles. "That meant she was scrambling to find all the paperwork and provide all the information that the buyer wanted. She also said she felt like the buyer took advantage of her because it was clear she wasn't prepared. She said she wished she had done a QofE early, and she wished she had identified solutions to potential problems early so she could present her business in the best possible light. She didn't, though, and it showed in the final offer she got from the buyer."

"That makes sense," Hiroshi replied. "I'll do what I can to start preparing, but that's definitely something that I'll prioritize discussing with whichever sell-side advisor I hire."

NEGOTIATING THE FINAL AGREEMENTS AND CLOSING THE DEAL

ANDY

O NCE YOU'RE THROUGH THE DUE DILIGENCE process, the end is in sight. But there's one more crucial component in the sale process: negotiating the final agreements, particularly the purchase agreement.

Negotiations around the purchase agreement—which can typically take anywhere from thirty to sixty days to complete—should begin when 80 to 90 percent of the due diligence process is complete. That's when the buyer has a great enough understanding of the company to draft a good, comprehensive agreement.

No matter what industry you're in, the purchase agreement has three important areas that I'd like to discuss: the representations and warranties, the indemnification provisions, and details about the deal structure (from how rollovers are handled and earnouts are structured, to how the seller note is set up, and every legality in between).

Like diligence, purchase agreement negotiations are complex, highly nuanced, and beyond the scope of this book to describe completely. However, I think it's worth taking a high-level look at what goes into this part of the sale process, so you can better prepare yourself to achieve a successful outcome.

A quick note before we dive in: In most sales, the buyer provides the initial draft of the purchase agreement. Regardless of whether it's provided by the buyer or the seller, though, there are three main ways these agreements are initially positioned. The first is very buyer-friendly, the second is very seller-friendly (if provided by the seller), and the third splits the difference. Of these, the first two—overly buyer-friendly and overly seller-friendly—are red flags. In my experience, the best initial purchase agreement proposals strike a balance between both parties.

DISCLOSE EVERYTHING

One of the most important elements of the purchase agreement is what's known as the representations and warranties.

Essentially, these are claims the seller makes about the status and condition of each element of their business.

I coach our clients—and I'm going to give you the same advice—to disclose everything possible to the buyer in the purchase agreement. Is there a potential environmental situation? Disclose it. A lawsuit with an employee? Disclose it. A customer who has indicated they will cease doing business with you? Disclose it. In fact, *over*-disclose. Doing so will help protect you from any claims by the buyer post-sale and ensure you receive all the funds due to you.

There are multiple categories a seller needs to disclose in the representations and warranties, including but not limited to:

- Accounts Receivable and Accounts Payable
- Books and Records
- Capitalization
- Compliance with Legal
- Contracts
- Customers and Suppliers
- Debt
- Employees
- Financials
- Governing Documents
- Intellectual Property
- Real Property

Along with these categories (which I've listed in alphabetical order), the purchase agreement includes schedules to back up each area of disclosure, document the state and condition of the company, and describe what assets—such as intellectual property, accounts payable, accounts receivable, and so on—are and are not included. On top of that, the schedules might also describe the company's top ten customers for the last two years, its top ten suppliers for the past two years, and so on.

In many cases, a portion of the seller's proceeds (generally 5 to 10 percent of the deal, depending on the size of the transaction) are put in an indemnification "holdback" account and held in escrow for twelve to twenty-four months post-close. This protects the buyer in case any claims come up that need to be addressed. For example, let's say the seller stated they fully paid their sales tax across all states in which they do business. However, in the year after closing, the buyer discovers the seller made a mistake and *didn't* pay all their taxes. The buyer can make a claim and then pay the overdue taxes and penalties out of the indemnification fund. And of course, if no claims arise by the time the escrow period ends, the money gets released from the fund to the seller.

There are a few exceptions to this rule. If a seller commits fraud, no matter how long ago it was, the buyer can make a claim against that. And the same is true for taxes prior to closing: There's no survival period, so as the seller, you are responsible for paying overdue taxes even if the indemnification period is over.

To help the buyer and seller manage the potential claims post-close and minimize conflicts, you can get something called rep and warranty insurance. *This insurance—which is relatively affordable—covers any claims that are made. There are a few benefits to going this route. First, the insurance takes the place of the escrow account (or covers a significant portion of it), which means the seller gets more of their money faster. Second, if there's a claim, insurance handles it, which means the buyer and seller can avoid any legal disputes. As you can imagine, this is especially helpful if the seller stays on after closing.*

Rep and warranty insurance can be negotiated as part of the purchase agreement. Define who will pay for it (many times, the buyer pays, but I have seen some instances where the cost is split between the buyer and the seller) and who will pay the deductible (generally the buyer). Also, keep in mind that the insurance company will do their own due diligence before issuing the insurance policy. That process generally doesn't add much time to the sale process because it's done simultaneously with the purchase agreement negotiations, but it's still something to be aware of. On top of that, the insurance company may find certain liabilities (i.e., known environmental liabilities that have been disclosed) and decide to exclude them from the policy.

Bottom line, the rep and warranty insurance might not cover everything, but it can still be beneficial for both the buyer and seller if the deal is substantial enough.

In some instances, the buyer may identify things in their due diligence that are materially significant to what they were initially told. In those cases, they may choose to address those items in the purchase agreement negotiations by changing the deal structure. I recently worked with a client who experienced this. They had more concentration with a large customer than the buyer originally thought. The buyer was willing to move forward with the deal, but they put an earnout in the deal structure for the customer to be kept on for two more years with at least the same level of revenue. With this updated deal structure, the seller has the opportunity to make the same amount of deal proceeds, but they have to help make sure that customer at least stays stable.

ADDRESS WORKING CAPITAL

Along with the reps and warranties, it's important to negotiate how working capital will be treated. Sellers can leave a lot of money on the table if they don't understand this part of the purchase agreement, so let's go through it in some detail so you're prepared.

Almost every buyer requires a normalized level of working capital (current assets minus current liabilities, excluding cash and debt) for the business to continue. That normalized amount is defined in the purchase price as the *target working capital*, or the amount of working capital estimated to be in the business at close.

Let's say that the target working capital is averaged to $2 million. That number will be noted in the purchase agreement, but because business is dynamic, approximately three days prior to closing, another estimate will be prepared with what you *think* the working capital is at closing. For the sake of the example, we'll say that the estimate is $1.9 million. Because the estimate is $100,000 less than the target, there's a corresponding reduction of $100,000 in the purchase price the buyer pays (this is known as a *purchase price adjustment*).

Sixty to ninety days post-close, the buyer's accountant will perform an audit to true up how much working capital was actually delivered versus the estimate. Again, for illustrative purposes, imagine that $1.75 million of working capital was delivered. In that case, another $125,000 will go back to the buyer to account for that discrepancy (generally, the adjustment is taken from the indemnification fund or from a special working capital escrow fund).

Of course, it can go the other way, too—if the true-up reveals that more working capital was delivered than estimated, the buyer will have to make that up to the seller. However, I hope that from the above example, you can see how getting working capital wrong can cost you money. Another example to drive the point home: Let's say your target is $2.5 million, but your pre-close estimate of working capital is $2 million. At that point, the buyer will reduce the purchase price by $500,000 (target minus the estimate). Now imagine that when the true-up happens, it's clear that the $2 million estimate correctly reflected the working capital at the time of closing. If you were in this situation as the seller, you would have taken a half-million-dollar reduction in the purchase price for your company, all because you got the target wrong.

If you have a solid quality of earnings report, it should be relatively easy to figure out target working capital, but since there's potentially so much money on the line here, my recommendation is to work closely with your accounting firm and your sell-side advisor to come up with your working capital target and estimate. Ideally, your target and estimate should match the working capital you deliver to the buyer to the penny so that no adjustments are needed anywhere along the way.

I should mention that I have seen some deals where the buyer and seller agree that as long as the estimate is within a certain dollar amount of what's delivered (i.e., $50,000), then no adjustments are made. However, it's much more common for the purchase agreement to require the estimate to match exactly how much working capital is delivered; if it doesn't, an adjustment will be made.

Almost all deals are cash-free/debt-free, so any cash on the books goes to the seller. Similarly, if there are any long-term loans or lines of credit on the business, they will get paid off at close, so the buyer gets a business that's free and clear of all long-term debts.

KEEP YOUR FOOT ON THE GAS

It generally takes about sixty days for both sides to negotiate all the details and finalize the purchase agreement. Couple that with the fact that you have already spent months on the sale process, and it's understandable that most sellers (and buyers, for that matter) are exhausted and just want to get everything done.

This is another stage where the deal can derail, because everyone is tired and the negotiations can get emotional. That's why it's so important as a seller to make sure your lawyers are focused on getting a good strategic deal done and that you have a strong sell-side advisor in your corner who will manage the lawyers to help smooth over any bumps in the road and keep the lawyers from wrecking the deal.

During this stage of the process, our firm spends a lot of time figuring out what points are truly important to our clients, and which are less so. That way, we can make sure the deal keeps moving forward and doesn't blow up over something that doesn't really matter. A good example of this—and something I see fairly often—are negotiations around noncompetes. Many buyers want the noncompete clause to remain in effect for five years. That can trigger a lot of sellers, because they often think it should be for a shorter period of time. What we remind them, though, is that if they are getting a huge sum of money for their company *and* they don't plan to compete with the buyer anyway (or at least potentially for multiple years), then writing the purchase agreement with a five-year noncompete actually feels reasonable.

The best piece of advice I can give you for getting through these negotiations successfully is to keep your foot on the gas, trust the process, and maintain your momentum. Lean on your advisor if you need to, but don't let exhaustion derail you. Remember, by the time you get to the purchase agreement negotiations, the finish line is in sight.

Once the purchase agreement is complete, it's normal to do a simultaneous sign and close. In those instances, the agreement is signed and the funds are wired the same day. Sometimes, though, there are contingencies to closing after signing. As an example, the buyer might need to meet the key customers, the seller might need to get shareholder approval, or regulatory approvals might be required for the transaction. In these instances, the agreement will get signed and the close will take place at an agreed-upon later date to give all parties time to complete the needed contingencies.

Upon closing, the buyer will instruct their bank to release the funds to the seller. There's a very detailed worksheet called a *funds flow* worksheet that lists every person/entity (shareholders, employees, debt holders, lawyers, and advisors to the deal process) who will receive funds from the transaction. The worksheet will include each party's name, contact information, and bank account details. To avoid cyber fraud, those details are double- or triple-checked *and* verbally verified by phone. Once everything is verified, funds usually hit the seller's account within twenty-four hours (if both parties are in the United States), or within a few days if either party is international.

Once the funds are in your account, it's customary to notify the buyers that you've received the funds. At that point, you can pop the champagne: You've sold your business, and it's time to celebrate!

CHARLES AND HIROSHI

Picking up his phone, Charles quickly dialed Hiroshi.

"Hi, Charles!"

"Hiroshi!" Charles said. "I just realized that we never talked about the very last step in the sale process:

negotiating the purchase agreement. By the time you get to that point, you're probably going to be exhausted. Make sure you lean on your advisor to help you stay grounded, and work closely with them and your accounting team to figure out your working capital. Oh, and remind your lawyer that they need to avoid getting into conflict over points that don't matter or don't help you. Instead, they should stay laser-focused on getting that good strategic deal done."

"That makes a lot of sense, Charles," Hiroshi said. "Thanks so much for that advice. I know I've said it before, but it seems like having the right team is crucial for every step of the process. Thanks to my conversations with you and Alma, I'm starting to build that great team. I can't wait to see where we end up!"

"I think you'll be really happy, Hiroshi," Charles responded. "Oh! And one more thing while we're on the subject. It's really important that you disclose everything about your company—the good, the bad, and the ugly—when you're working on the reps and warranties. That's the best way to avoid potential claims from the buyer."

"What sort of things should I disclose?" Hiroshi asked.

"That's something your sell-side advisor can help you with, but the rule of thumb my advisor taught me was to over-disclose everything. For example, we had an environmental situation that had the potential to cause some problems down the road. Even though it might have been fine, my advisor recommended that we disclose it just in case. Err on the side of caution and protect yourself by disclosing every issue and potential issue up front."

"That's good advice," Hiroshi said. "We're in a lawsuit with an employee right now that seems like it might drag on for a long time. That's something else I should disclose when we get to that stage, I guess."

"Definitely," Charles responded. "You can also look into getting rep and warranty insurance. It'll add a little more complexity to the process because the insurance company will do their own due diligence, but it's pretty affordable and can help avoid conflicts down the road, especially if you're planning to continue working with the buyer after they acquire your company."

"Thanks, Charles," Hiroshi said. "I'll definitely look into the insurance, and I'll make sure to disclose every single thing that might be an issue. Better safe than sorry, after all!"

THIRTEEN

GOING FROM SALE TO POST-SALE

JONATHAN

SELLING A BUSINESS IS LIFE-CHANGING, BUT what happens after the wire transfer clears? Many entrepreneurs make the mistake of focusing solely on closing the deal and fail to prepare for what comes next—not just emotionally, but financially.

Before my sale was finalized, my business coach connected me with a highly regarded financial advisory firm. I started meeting with them months before closing, which gave me time to plan my post-sale finances properly. One of my biggest concerns was ensuring financial privacy. The last thing I wanted was to deposit a large sum into a local bank where word might spread. People talk, especially in a small town, and I didn't want unnecessary attention on my finances. My wealth advisors helped me establish appropriate banking structures so that when the deal closed, the funds were transferred securely and discreetly.

Another priority was setting up a trust for my daughter. If something happened to me or my wife, I needed to make sure that our financial assets were protected and properly allocated. With the guidance of my wealth advisors, I worked with a highly qualified estate attorney to establish a comprehensive trust. This allowed me to make decisions ahead of any potential emergencies, rather than leaving things to be sorted out in court or through family disputes.

Once the sale was complete, we also had to figure out investment strategies and cash flow management. I no longer had a salary, so we worked with our advisors to determine how much we needed to live on, what level of investment risk we were comfortable with, and how to structure our portfolio for long-term sustainability.

> *Pro tip: Start working with a wealth advisor as early in the process as possible—ideally before you start working with a sell-side advisor. Figuring out how much you need to support your and your family's lifestyle post-sale is crucial when it comes to determining the minimum amount you can sell your company for.*

A major financial decision my wife and I made was setting up a donor-advised fund (DAF) before the sale. This allowed us to donate a portion of our proceeds while also significantly reducing our tax burden. We are firm believers in tithing, so this was a perfect solution for us. By setting up the DAF in advance, we were able to essentially reduce our tax liability twice as much as we would have if we had donated to charity without setting up the DAF. Plus, because a DAF allows you to distribute funds over time to charities, rather than requiring an immediate lump-sum donation, we had the flexibility to prayerfully and strategically decide where to give, rather than rushing the decision.

The right financial team can make all the difference in making sure that the proceeds from a lifetime of hard work are safeguarded, optimized, and aligned with personal and family goals. Just as you must carefully choose the right buyer for your business, you must also carefully choose the right legal and financial advisors for your future.

TAKE STEPS TO AVOID REGRET POST-SALE

I've talked to some sellers who have told me they had regrets post-sale. If that happens, it might help to remind yourself that you sold the buyer a great business. What they do with it after the sale is out of your hands. That's an important mindset for any entrepreneur to adopt. *When you sell, you need to fully commit to the decision and let go.* If the new owners mismanage the business, that's on them—not on you. You built something valuable, and you earned the outcome. Don't dwell on what happens next. Be proud of what you accomplished.

One of the biggest challenges is realizing that if the same level of vision, drive, and leadership that built the company isn't maintained after the sale, the business may not achieve its projected growth or even sustain past success. The grit and determination that entrepreneurs bring to their companies must be replaced by someone equally committed. Otherwise, expectations will not be met.

With that said, many times, the new owners take the company to new heights. This is why you absolutely must choose the *right* buyer, not just the highest offer—especially if you're staying on in some capacity or have earnouts built into the deal. Remember, enthusiasm for the company's mission must continue under new ownership, or the business will struggle. Many sellers assume that once the deal is finalized, the company's future is secured. The truth is, its fate depends on who is at the helm.

Once I made the decision to move forward with the strategic buyer I've told you about and signed the LOI, I never looked back. If you're still waffling between options after signing, that's usually a sign you made the decision too soon or didn't take enough time to weigh all the factors. At the same time, you can't drag the process out indefinitely. Your advisor will guide you, but buyers won't wait around forever.

GET READY FOR A NEW IDENTITY

Selling a business is often framed as the ultimate goal, but what few entrepreneurs talk about is what happens next. After years of grinding, building, and making the business a core part of their identity, the sudden shift to not running a company anymore can be disorienting.

For twenty-six years, my life was about growth and forward motion. I had been a president, an owner, and a leader in my industry. There was no "arrival"—only the next challenge, the next goal, the next deal. Work wasn't just what I did. It was a major part of who I was.

Then, one day, it was over.

The moment the wire transfer went through, I stared at the banking app on my phone and saw the balance update. The deal was done. But instead of feeling overwhelming excitement, I felt...quiet. There weren't going to be any more emails. There weren't going to be any more phone calls, or any urgent fires to put out. I was no longer needed, and that realization hit harder than I expected.

For years prior to selling Quicken Steel, I had watched as other entrepreneurs—colleagues, friends, and so on—sold their companies and immediately jumped into the next venture.

Instead of giving themselves time after exiting, they got back into the fray, buying businesses, making investments, and diving back into the grind. I understood the temptation; post-sale restlessness is real. There's an urge to keep moving, keep building, keep proving your worth. But I had been strongly advised to take at least a year off before making any major decisions.

That pause changed everything. At first, I struggled with the absence of busyness. For the first time in my life, I had no pressing deadlines, no financial pressure, no urgent decisions to make. I started taking long walks, reflecting on what life looked like without a company to run. Without the daily hustle, who was I?

Initially, it caused me some anxiety, but over time, I realized that stillness wasn't something to be feared. Rather, it was an opportunity. Instead of immediately diving into another high-pressure business venture, I decided to listen. To be prayerful. To let what was next unfold naturally instead of forcing my way forward.

That led me to unexpected places. I have always loved being a father, but suddenly I had the luxury to be even more present for my daughter. It was incredibly rewarding being free to take care of Faith, and ensuring she was getting the best care—not to mention spending quality time with her— was a dream come true.

Other things started to emerge, too. For one, I started working on this book. The idea had been in the back of my mind for a while, but I wasn't sure if I had anything valuable to say. But in the quiet moments, the thought kept returning—not as a loud, urgent idea, but as a steady, persistent pull. Then, I started getting invited to speak at business events focused on helping entrepreneurs who were in the process of selling their businesses. Each time I spoke, the audiences of business owners asked me questions, all of which seemed to follow a common thread. I realized writing a book could help address those questions for people who wanted to exit but might not be able to get to a seminar about it. When I finally spoke with Andy about joining me in co-authoring this book, everything fell into place. It was the right time, the right project, and the right way to use my experience to help others.

Today, I'm still working on projects and staying involved in various ventures, but my perspective has shifted. I no longer feel the need to define my worth by constant movement. Instead, I focus on what truly matters, and on letting things unfold instead of forcing them to happen.

For anyone transitioning out of a business, the emotional shift is just as important as the financial one. Once the deal is done, your sense of identity will change, and you have to be intentional about finding a new sense of purpose—not just a new business venture, but something that truly fulfills you.

For me, that has meant learning to be still, to trust, and to let life unfold in its own time. That's not always easy for me, because my entire professional life was built around charging forward and making things happen. It's an ongoing journey, but one I'm finally embracing. And from where I'm sitting, it's clear: Selling your business isn't the end—it's just the beginning of something new.

HIROSHI

As he hung up the phone, Hiroshi couldn't stop smiling. He had done it—he had hired a dedicated sell-side advisor...one who ticked all the boxes that Charles and Alma had mentioned. He knew he had a long way to go, but after doing everything he could to make sure that both he and his company were prepared for what was coming, he was excited. Hiring an advisor felt like a major step in a long list of preparatory actions he had taken, and he was confident it would reap massive rewards.

As he grabbed his coat and walked out of his office, he let his mind drift to what life would be like *after* the sale. He knew that Charles was loving life and fulfilling his dream of traveling with his wife and family. Alma, on the other hand, wasn't as happy.

Hiroshi decided to see if Charles had any advice for him about how to make the transition from sale to post-sale. After all, just like with everything else related to the sale process, it seemed like preparing early might be the key to a successful outcome.

FOURTEEN

LIFE AFTER THE DEAL

ANDY

A
S YOU APPROACH THE FINAL DECISION IN YOUR
M&A transaction, you're going to face one of the most
important moments of your entire entrepreneurial
journey: *choosing the right buyer.* Remember, for most
sellers, this isn't merely a "numbers" decision. You need
to choose the buyer who aligns best with your personal and
business goals, ensures a good home for employees, continues your legacy, and offers a deal that delivers on both financial and strategic fronts.

Before you make your decision, the first and most critical
step is to revisit your original motivations for selling. Recall
why you are pursuing this transaction. What outcomes are
required (your *must-haves*), and which are preferred (your

nice-to-haves)? Every offer should be evaluated against these core objectives. Carefully identify which offers best align with your goals and make sure your expectations, both financial and operational, are met.

CONSIDER YOUR MOTIVATIONS
WHEN EVALUATING OFFERS

Sellers often face a choice between financial buyers and strategic buyers. Each type of buyer presents distinct advantages and potential challenges.

Remember, *financial buyers* are typically private equity firms or investment groups that are focused on acquiring businesses as investments. To further that goal, they may scale the company through additional capital and operational efficiencies. For example, in one case, Jonathan was presented with an offer from a financial buyer who wanted to replicate his business model in multiple new regions. The buyer's strategy was to finance growth through grassroots expansion rather than integrating the business into an existing supply chain. However, while the offer was strong financially, it may have lacked the operational synergies that would have ensured long-term success for the business and its employees.

Strategic buyers, on the other hand, seek acquisitions that complement each business for transformative mutual growth—where 1+1 = 3, 4, 5, or more. They seek businesses whose growth they can accelerate, while the acquired business also helps them build a stronger mutual competitive advantage.

Once you decide which type of buyer to focus on, three key factors should guide your final decision:

Key Factors to Decide on a Buyer

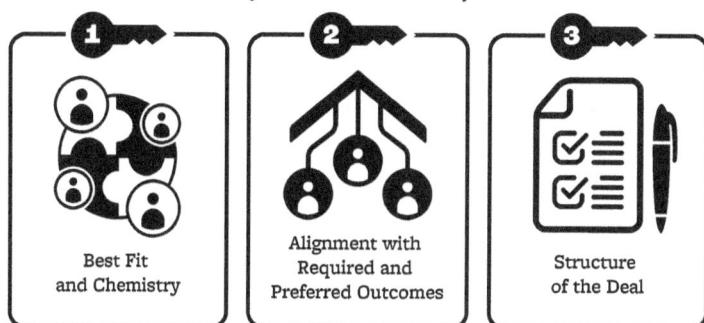

1	2	3
Best Fit and Chemistry	Alignment with Required and Preferred Outcomes	Structure of the Deal

1. **Fit and Chemistry**: The best deals are not merely transactional but involve relationships. Consider your personal rapport with potential buyers. Are the buyers trustworthy? Do they share similar values? Will they preserve the company culture and support the team post-acquisition? Chemistry is often a deciding factor when multiple offers appear financially comparable.

2. **Alignment with Required and Preferred Outcomes:** Stay grounded in your original goals. If an offer checks

all the necessary boxes, whether financial security, operational continuity, or personal legacy, then it is a strong contender.

3. **Structure of the Deal**: The financial terms of an offer go beyond just the purchase price. Is the offer all cash, or does it include rollover equity or an earnout? What are the tax implications of the deal structure? Will you remain involved post-sale, and if so, under what terms?

Once you select a buyer, the deal enters an *exclusivity period*. This phase indicates that there is a commitment from both parties, and it allows the buyer to conduct extensive due diligence. As we discussed earlier, during this period, the buyer will invest significant resources (e.g., hiring third-party legal, tax, industry, and accounting professionals) to verify everything you have represented and confirm the strategic potential of the acquisition.

You need to be prepared for an intense phase of scrutiny that will require you to manage multiple work streams simultaneously. Stay responsive to the buyer and lean on your sell-side advisor to facilitate a smooth process. Any surprises discovered during due diligence, such as customer issues, operational deficiencies, shareholder issues, unpaid sales taxes, or compliance issues, must be resolved collaboratively, often through indemnifications, deal structuring adjustments, or financial holdbacks.

Remember, the process of selecting a buyer is as much about the cultural and strategic fit as it is about financial gain. By maintaining clarity on your objectives, understanding the nuances between financial and strategic buyers, and preparing for the due diligence phase, you can navigate this complex decision with confidence. With the right guidance and a clear vision, you can help ensure that the business you've built continues to thrive under new ownership.

PLAN FOR LIFE AFTER THE DEAL

Finally, one of the most overlooked aspects of selling a business is planning for what comes next. Many owners focus intensely on the mechanics of the sale—such as due diligence, legal negotiations, and financial outcomes—but give little thought to their personal transition. What happens after the ink dries?

As Jonathan discussed earlier, you need to be prepared for life post-sale. I always put my clients through an exercise we call "The Owner's Outcome," which is built around answering two key questions:

1. What are your personal and professional goals *before* the exit?

2. What are your personal and professional goals *after* the exit?

These questions sound simple, but they are incredibly powerful in shaping a seller's mindset before the transaction begins. Some entrepreneurs sell their business and immediately feel a sense of accomplishment, seeing it as the reward for years of hard work. Others struggle with the transition, feeling lost without their daily purpose.

If you're staying on after you sell, it's important to remember that selling a business means shifting from being the sole decision-maker to reporting to someone else, whether that's a corporate acquirer, private equity firm, or new ownership team. Many founders underestimate how difficult that change can be. Suddenly, they are no longer the ultimate authority, and that shift in identity can be challenging.

The most successful transitions happen when business owners develop a clear vision for their life during *and* after the sale. I recommend creating a vision board to paint a vivid picture of what life will look like for you, your family, your community, your business, and so on in the first year, five years, and beyond. Questions to consider include:

- How will you turn this success into significance?
- Where will you live?
- What will your role be in the business, if any?

- How will you spend time with your spouse, children, or grandchildren?
- What will you do in your community, with your faith, or in charitable work?
- What hobbies, travel, or health goals will you pursue?
- Will you start another business, and if so, on what timeline?

Being intentional and specific about post-exit life is incredibly important. Instead of vague ideas like "spend more time with family," successful sellers outline concrete goals: "Take three vacations a year with my spouse and two trips with my kids or grandkids." If they plan to stay active in the business world, they set targets like "launch a new company within twenty-four months." And if they are philanthropically minded, they don't say something like "give to charity." Instead, they make that goal specific, too: "Give 10 percent of profit to charity over a five-year period." No matter what goals you have, getting really granular about them will ease the transition to life post-sale.

As you create your vision board, make sure your spouse, family members, and other key stakeholders are aligned with this vision. Major life transitions don't affect just you. They impact your entire family. Getting buy-in from those closest to you can help create a sense of accountability and ensure a smoother transition.

By going through the owner's outcome and vision board exercises early, ideally before even beginning the sale process, you will gain the clarity you need to move forward confidently. And you will be able to step into the next chapter of your life with purpose.

From Success to Significance—how does your life become more meaningful and purposeful as a result of this sale? By answering that question before the deal closes, you will set yourself up for not just a successful sale, but a more fulfilling life afterward.

CHARLES AND HIROSHI

"Hey, Hiroshi!" Charles said into his phone. "What can I do for you, my friend?"

"I just hired a sell-side advisor!" Hiroshi said. "This is getting real!"

"Congratulations!"

"Thanks. But something occurred to me that I wanted to ask you about. I know you've really been enjoying life post-sale. You've had such great advice about how I can prepare for other parts of the sale process. Do you have any tips about how to make sure I thrive *after* my exit?"

"You ask all the right questions, Hiroshi," Charles replied. "That's one that your sell-side advisor—and your coach, if you have one—should definitely be able to help you with. But I can tell you that the number one thing that's helped me was mapping out my personal and professional goals before and after the exit. I got really granular about it, too. I knew that I wanted to move, and I knew *where* we wanted to be. I knew exactly how I wanted to spend time with my wife and kids, I knew I wanted to take time to improve my golf game, and I knew that I wanted to start another business after my noncompete ended. I talked everything over with my wife, too, because I knew this exit meant we could craft new lives together. Getting that level of detail gave my days purpose. It helped a lot."

"That's so helpful," Hiroshi said. "Thank you!"

"You're welcome, my friend," Charles replied. "I think your exit is going to be great. I'm rooting for you!"

CONCLUSION

YOUR EXIT, YOUR LEGACY

Selling a business is one of the most profound milestones in an entrepreneur's journey. It represents the culmination of years, possibly decades, of hard work, risk-taking, and leadership. It's also a complex, often emotional process that requires strategic foresight, meticulous preparation, and the right team of advisors.

We've covered a lot of ground in this book. However, if there's one overarching lesson we want to leave you with, it's this: *Don't go it alone.* Right alongside that, we have one other crucial piece of advice: *It's never too early to start preparing for your exit.*

A successful exit doesn't happen by accident. It's the result of careful and intentional planning. Whether your sale is a few months or a few years away, the work you do today will determine the outcome when that moment arrives.

First, understand the key value drivers of your business. Buyers, especially strategic buyers, will pay a premium for a business that is well structured and positioned for future growth, because it has the potential to transform *both* businesses. Take the time to organize your financials, streamline your operations, and build a leadership team that doesn't depend on you to function.

Beyond business fundamentals, preparation also includes things like tax planning, estate structuring, and wealth preservation. Too many sellers leave substantial money on the table simply because they didn't take the time to optimize their financial and legal frameworks ahead of a sale. Early action leads to better financial outcomes.

HIRE THE RIGHT ADVISOR

Most business owners are experts at running their companies, but selling a business is an entirely different skill set. Even if you've built a highly profitable enterprise, selling it requires specialized expertise. That's why hiring a specialized M&A sell-side advisor is so important (and why we keep reinforcing this issue). An experienced sell-side advisor doesn't just connect you with buyers. They manage the process, create competitive tension, negotiate the agreement(s), make sure that no money is left on the table, and get the deal closed. More importantly, they act as a buffer during negotiations, protecting you from unnecessary distractions and helping you navigate the emotional highs and lows of a deal.

Even a seasoned entrepreneur who has sold a business before will benefit from an advisor who can anticipate road-blocks and keep the deal moving forward. The right advisor will also help you avoid costly mistakes, such as underestimating due diligence demands, mispricing your business, getting into conflict with the buyer, or getting trapped in unfavorable deal terms. Ultimately, with all they bring to the table, the right advisor will more than pay for themselves.

PLAN FOR WHAT COMES NEXT

Before you sell, take the time to answer two critical questions:

1. Why am I selling?
2. What do I want to achieve?

Some entrepreneurs sell to maximize their financial return. Others prioritize finding the right cultural fit, ensuring job security for employees, or securing their company's long-term legacy. Whatever your reasons, having clear required and preferred outcomes ensures that your sale aligns with both your business and personal goals.

Just as important is knowing what life will look like after the sale. The transition from business owner to *former* business owner can be jarring. One day, you're making key decisions and driving the company forward. The next, you wake up without a full calendar or a clear sense of purpose.

We've both seen it time and time again. Some sellers embrace the change and view it as their hard-earned reward, while others struggle to find meaning after the exit. The ones who make this transition best are the sellers who planned for life after the sale and had a clear vision in place.

Take the time to define your next chapter. Where will you live? How will you spend your time? What will give you purpose? Whether it's traveling with family, getting involved in philanthropy, starting a new venture, or focusing on health and wellness, creating a vision for your future will make the transition smoother and more fulfilling.

OWN YOUR EXIT

We'll say it one more time. If you're considering selling your business, take the time to prepare now. If that means delaying the sale by six months, a year, or even several years to build out your team, surround yourself with an A-team of external advisors, optimize your company's financials, strengthen its operations, and/or secure a better tax position, *do it*. The extra effort will pay dividends in the valuation and deal terms buyers are willing to offer, not to mention your post-sale experience.

Ultimately, selling your business isn't just about financial gain. It's about preserving your legacy, securing the best possible outcome, and setting yourself up for greater success and significance in the next phase of life. The entrepreneurs who achieve the best results are the ones who work with the right advisors, take preparation seriously, and approach the sale with strategic intent.

You built your business with purpose. By following the advice in this book, you'll be able to sell it with purpose, too.

APPENDIX

We know that the sale process has a lot of moving parts. So, we've prepared a Gantt chart of the key points in the sale timeline, using Quicken Steel as an example.

The timeline shows the thirteen-month sale process, starting from the point we started working together and ending when we closed our deal.

Sales Process Flow Chart for Quicken Steel

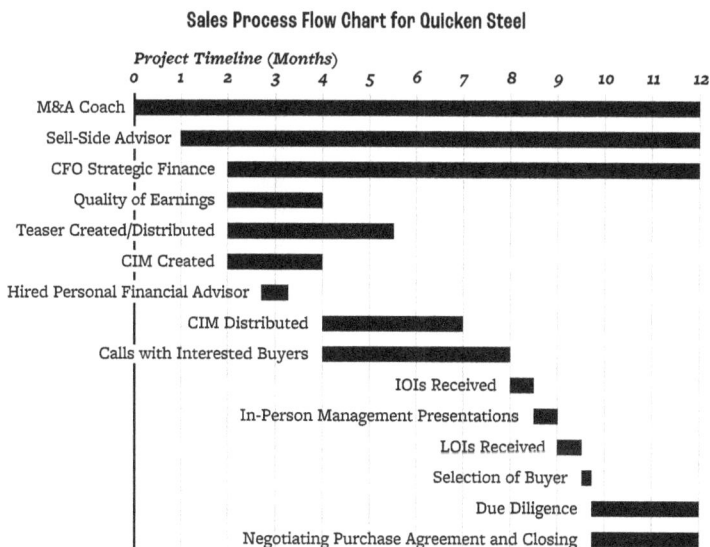

ACKNOWLEDGMENTS

JONATHAN

I want to begin by expressing my deepest gratitude to my parents, John and Carleena Sherrill—the truest examples of integrity and the most generous individuals I have ever known. Your unwavering belief in me laid the foundation for all my endeavors, and I am profoundly grateful to have been guided by your example.

To my wife, Dana, and our daughter, Faith—your love and support have been my anchor and my inspiration. You are the heart of my journey, and I am eternally thankful for your presence in my life.

To Andy Harris—my sell-side advisor and co-author of this book. Andy, your steadfast integrity and unwavering professionalism were instrumental during the sale of my business. Collaborating with you on this book has been invaluable, and your dedication to helping business owners navigate complex transitions shines through in these pages.

To Kristin Clark and the team at Elite Content Creation/ Cheval Press—thank you for your exceptional editorial support. Your keen eye and commitment to refining our manuscript ensured that our ideas were communicated clearly and effectively.

To my business coach, John Giegerich—your strategic insights kept me grounded during pivotal moments, steering my professional journey with wisdom.

To my life coach, Paul Thompson—thank you for constantly pointing me back to God. Your counsel helped me keep my priorities aligned with His will and reminded me of what truly matters.

To everyone who has been part of this journey—through conversations, encouragement, or simply being there—thank you. Your contributions, big and small, have been deeply appreciated.

ANDY

My deepest thanks to the many people who have supported me and contributed to my success, especially my loving wife, Stephanie, who offered valuable insights about my contributions to this book, and who has always been my biggest supporter.

I also want to thank my daughters, Hannah and Georgia, for their love and support. You are a key part of my purpose. I love you both so much.

Thank you to my co-author, Jonathan Sherrill, for partnering with me on this project. It's been an honor and a privilege to write this book with you.

To my late parents, Bonney and George, and my in-laws, Martha and George. Their impact on my character, my faith, and my approach to life continues to shape me to this day.

A huge thank-you to STS Capital Partners chairman and founder Rob Follows, who gives me the opportunity to live my *why* every day, and to all the team members in STS who support our clients in achieving Extraordinary Exits.

I owe a debt of gratitude to Arsenal Capital Partners and Edgewater Capital Partners. As a CEO for companies that were backed by these firms, I learned an incredible amount from the people at both firms about how to successfully lead and build teams and businesses to achieve strategic exits. The impact both organizations had on my career is greater than I can ever express.

Finally, I want to acknowledge and thank the Young Presidents' Organization (YPO). I've been a member for many years. In that time, I've learned invaluable lessons, met amazing people, and grown in my career.

ABOUT THE AUTHORS

Entrepreneur, investor, and M&A strategist **Jonathan Sherrill** scaled and sold businesses for nearly twenty years. Today, Jonathan invests in business ventures. An author and speaker, he also provides CEO coaching services, helping business owners achieve their goals and prepare for successful exits. He and his family call Florida home.

Andy Harris is a proven CEO and M&A sell-side advisor with three decades of leadership experience. As president of North American Strategies and managing director at STS Capital Partners, Andy expertly guides clients through all phases of the M&A process, helping business owners achieve eight- and nine-digit exits. He lives in California and works globally.

www.ingramcontent.com/pod-product-compliance
Lightning Source LLC
Chambersburg PA
CBHW031848200326
41597CB00012B/319